FOUNDATIONS OF THE FAITH

GOD, CHRIST, AND THE CHURCH

JEFF VEHIGE

FIND THE FAITH

To my parents, Ron and Elaine.

Because of my father's ultimatum when I was nineteen ("Attend Mass on Sundays, or move out") and my mother's nudge a few days later ("There's this college Bible study at church you might like"), I'm a Catholic who found the faith.

To believe is nothing other than to think with assent. Believers are also thinkers: in believing, they think and in thinking, they believe. If faith does not think, it is nothing.

— SAINT AUGUSTINE OF HIPPO

CONTENTS

As the title implies, the *Find the Faith* series is dedicated to helping people—Catholics in particular—find the truth of Christ our Lord and the Church he established. In this Preface (which opens every book in the series), I'd like to say a little about this apostolate.

In short, it's a series of books, along with an accompanying podcast, that walks through the four pillars of the Catholic faith—the creed, the sacraments, morality, and prayer. This fourfold division, rooted in the apostolic Church itself (Acts 2:42), has been used by the Church's two official catechisms: the *Roman Catechism*, published in 1566, and the *Catechism of the Catholic Church*, published in 1992.

But *Find the Faith* is more than a simple walk through Catholic teaching. I want to help you grasp something of the theological, philosophical, biblical, and historical background of Catholic doctrine and worship. I want to explore the relationship between doctrine and morality, and how both should penetrate our spiritual life. Why so much detail? One very simple reason.

Jesus said, "If you continue in my word ... you will know the truth, and the truth will make you free" (John 8:31). Truth cannot be skirted-over, dumbed-down, or diluted. It must be presented in its fullness. To teach adults as if they were children—which, in my experience, happens in many adult-level faith formation classes—is a grave injustice. This does not mean that the presentation of theology must be scholarly, academic, or snobbishly intellectual. Truth is a common good—a good given to all of us by God—and it should be accessible to anyone who wants to work for it. I hope to make the fullness of truth as accessible as possible without making it feel like you're reading a graduate-level theology book.

All of this begs the question: What gives me the authority to write such a work? Although I grew up in a Catholic family, I was a kid formed by the pagan-like culture of the 1980s. I didn't embrace the religion in which I was raised until I was in my late teens. Living in Los Angeles with dreams of becoming a professional musician (I played the guitar), I had a conversion experience in a West Hollywood Bible church (long story!). I moved back home to Texas a few months later, just after my nineteenth birthday, and was soon involved in a Catholic Bible study geared toward college students. A year later (this would have been 1994, during the fall) we took a break from Scripture to read Frank Sheed's *Theology for Beginners*. This book changed my life. Because of it, I read other theology books, poured over Sacred Scripture, consumed Scott Hahn tapes like a man dying of starvation (which I was; it was intellectual starvation), spent a year in a monastery, earned a BA in theology and then an MA in theology (both from the University of Dallas, a small Catholic liberal arts college), considered pursuing a PhD in theology, taught sacramental preparation classes for ten years at my parish, RCIA for seven years, Catechist Formation Classes for the Dioceses of Dallas for six, all while leading numerous parish-level theology classes, Bible studies, and more than a few reading groups. *Find the Faith* is the result of nearly twenty years of teaching theology at the parish level.

Along with the books, there is an accompanying podcast. The podcast is *not* an audio version of the books. Rather, it's a "lecture-style" presentation: I teach the same material, but do so as if I were in a classroom. My rationale to present the same material in two ways is simple: I want to reach as many people as possible. Not everyone is a reader, and not everyone has time to read. I'm a reader, but since my early twenties, my most reliable classroom has been my car. A podcast makes it possible for anyone who has the inclination to learn more about Catholicism to do so. It's free. It's portable. And since each *Find the Faith* episode is between forty and sixty minutes, it's bite-size.

Finally, I want to speak to the structure of this book. It's not often you read a book written in Q&A format. I first considered this format back in the spring of 2015, when I conceived the *Find the Faith* apostolate. I immediately rejected it as hokey. After all, the Q&A format implies a conversation is taking place. But this wouldn't be a *real* conversation; I would be making up the whole thing in order to write what I wanted to write. On the other hand, wouldn't I be writing what I wanted to write whether I made up questions or not?

Two years later, and after several failed drafts of the same book, I returned to the Q&A format for one rather ironic reason: I wanted better control of writing what I wanted to write. When talking about theology, I have an incredible proclivity to go down almost any rabbit hole that crosses my path. I discovered this to be especially true when writing, when I don't have the befuddled looks of students to lead me back to the discussion at hand. My tendency to pursue tangents vanished when I started playing around with the Q&A format. It took me out of the solitary act of writing and put me in a classroom setting. It forced me to keep a conversational tone instead of a technical, academic one. In a word, it reminded me of you, the reader.

And you, the reader, *should* be the primary focus. In the Parable of the Sower, the Lord tells us that only those who *understand* the faith will bear fruit (Matthew 13:23). That is my hope and prayer: that through the *Find the Faith* apostolate, you come to understand the truth of Jesus Christ and the Church he established. For only through understanding the faith can we know God; only in knowing God can we love him; only in loving him can we serve him. And it is only in serving God in love that we can bear fruit in this life—and the next.

January 21, 2018
Feast of Saint Agnes

INTRODUCTION

The Foundations of the Faith—that's the title of this book. And its subtitle is *God, Christ, and the Church.* The title is not the most attractive one in the world, and neither is the subtitle. But both work because they tell you exactly what this book is about.

What is a foundation? The dictionary tells us that a foundation is the "lowest load-bearing part of a building." It's that part of a building which holds all of the weight. Metaphorically, we might say that a mother is the foundation of her family, a quarterback is the foundation of the offense, or a secretary is the foundation of an administration. In each of these cases, it's the mother, the quarterback, or the secretary who bear the load—who carry the weight—of the others.

What is faith? As we'll discuss later, faith has two elements: (1) it's trusting the word of another (2) to the point of accepting what he says to be true and real.

But we do not blindly accept whatever someone tells us about anything; there must be a reason for us to have faith in another. We don't accept the medical advice of any person we meet on the street, but we do believe what our doctor tells us—even if we've never met him before. What are the foundations of our faith in our doctor? The reviews we read on the Internet. That he's associated with a major health care system in the area. And, of course, our first impression of him.

What is true for our faith in a doctor is true for our faith in anyone we meet, for any nonfiction book we read, for any teacher to whom we listen. There are reasons we have faith in this person, this book, this teacher. And so we can add a third element to the nature of faith. Faith is (1) trusting the word of another (2) to the point of accepting what he says to be true and real, but to put faith in another, we must have (3) a reason to do so.

In other words, faith is something we give once we have decided that faith is a reasonable, rational decision. Therefore, the reasons for faith can be seen as foundations—they bear the weight of faith itself.

If we ever find that we've lost faith in another person, it's not because faith itself was lost, but because the foundations that allowed us to believe were shaken, cracked, damaged. The wife who discovers her husband has cheated on her now has a reason *not* to trust, a foundation *not* to give him the assent of faith that she had once given him.

What is true for our faith in others is true for our faith in the Church. We believe the Church because we have reasons for believing. Unfortunately, many of these reasons are quite flimsy. "I was raised a Catholic," one will say. "I feel at home in the Church," another will say. "I like Pope Francis," a third will say. But these reasons are too weak to bear the weight of faith, and challenges expose their weakness. An anti-Catholic comment from a friend that has the ring of truth, a passage of Scripture that seems to run contrary to Catholic teaching, another report of a priest who abused the youth or a bishop who protected him—these are like explosives placed at the foundations of a building. They can damage solid foundations. Weak foundations don't stand a chance.

I have one goal for this book—to help you establish solid, bedrock foundations for your faith in God, in Christ, and in the Church. Faith needs reasons to be strong, and this book provides some of the reasons why it's rational to be a believing Catholic. This book is not about *what* you believe, but *why* you believe it.

And we focus on the *why* for one eminently practical reason: when challenges detonate around you, your faith will remain because it will have been built on solid foundations that can endure any explosion unscathed.

FAITH, REASON, AND ROCK-SOLID CONVICTIONS

It seems strange to open a book on God, Christ, and the Church with a discussion on faith and reason. Why did you begin here?

The late Father John Hardon once said, "We are only as strong as our minds are strong, and there's only one source of strength for the mind—and that is God's truth" (*Biblical Spirituality Retreat*, no. 002).

To accept God's truth, we must have faith. Faith in God, who is the source of truth. Faith in Christ, who is the fullness of God's truth. And faith in the Church, which is the guarantor of God's truth. Unfortunately, the word "faith" has been transformed to mean something it's never meant in Catholic theology, and this misunderstanding causes a lot of problems for anyone who wants to talk about what it means to believe.

The word comes from the Latin, *fides*, which means "trust" and "confidence." Most of the time "faith" is used correctly, such as when a man says, "I have faith in my wife." But other times the word is used incorrectly, such as when we hear a person say, "I'm a man of reason, not a man of faith." Is he saying that he's not a man of trust? That he lacks confidence in others? Of course not. But, then, what does he mean? Most likely, he means "easy of belief" or "easily believable." Now here's the problem: we already have an English word that means "easy of belief." It's "credulity." So a more precise way of speaking would be, "I'm a man of reason, not a credulous man." And as we all know, to trust someone is not the same thing as easily believing whatever he or she tells us.

But there's another problem with the statement "I'm a man of reason, not a man of faith." In this statement, "faith" always refers to *religious* belief. So what's really being said is this: "I'm a man of reason, not a religious man, for religious things are easily believable, and only credulous men can accept them as true." What does this added meaning do to the word "faith"? In a highly educated culture such as ours—in a culture dominated by math, science, and technology—it makes "faith" less than desirable, for who wants to be known as someone so weak of mind that he'll believe any half-baked idea presented to him?

Now, if it seems that I'm stretching things a bit, let me tell you about a conversation I had when I was still working on my undergraduate degree. This happened during a summer school biology class. For lab work, we were paired with another student, and when my partner found out I was majoring in theology, she said, "Oh, that must be easy." When I asked her why she thought that, she said, "Because it's about what you believe, which means you get to make everything up."

And so, before we can say anything about why we believe in God, in Christ, and in the Church, it seems logical to start by discussing the nature of faith, how faith relates to reason, and how a faith informed by reason gives us rock-solid convictions for being a committed Catholic.

Okay. So what *is* the nature of faith?

Faith is a way of truth. As John Paul II says, "Faith and reason are like two wings on which the human spirit rises to the truth" (Opening of *On Faith and Reason*). How is faith a way of truth? Because by faith we trust another and accept what he says to be true. Faith allows us to make the truth another possesses our own.

Our Lord asks, "When the Son of man comes, will he find faith on earth?" (Luke 18:8). What, exactly, is Jesus asking? He's asking this: Will he find the truth of God dwelling in the minds of men? Will he find people who believe what he has said, who have made his words their own, who act on that truth, who order their lives to it?

But the human mind does not simply receive truth and knowledge the way a glass receives water. When water is poured into a glass, the glass and the water remain separate. The water can be drunk, it can be poured out, or it can be left alone. In each case, the glass is completely unaltered by the water.

Not so with the human mind. When a thought enters it, the mind is affected. It cannot but be affected, for the mind is altered by what it knows. This is why we'll refuse to watch a movie or read a book—because we don't want certain thoughts in our mind! By nature, our intellects want to latch on to thoughts and ideas and begin a process that will lead to either accepting them as true or rejecting them as false. In this way, our intellects assimilate an idea, and it becomes our very own, part of our own mental landscape.

However, the mind does share one similarity with the glass: just as the glass awaits something outside of it to determine how the water will be used, the mind needs something outside of it to direct it. What is this something? It's the will, which is our freedom to choose. Now, the will doesn't determine how the mind will use an idea, for only the mind has the power to use an idea. But the will *does* determine if the mind will even consider the idea. In other words, we have power over our thoughts: we have the freedom to choose what we think about, and we have the freedom to choose what we ignore.

When we choose to think about an idea, we use our reason. The ancient Greek philosopher Aristotle (367–347 BC) said that "man is a rational animal." What did he mean? He meant that we have a mind that can understand the world around it. We are not simply experiencing and reacting to experiences. We can ponder, remember, imagine our experiences; we can learn from them. In a word, we can think.

When information is presented to us, we can judge new knowledge based on the body of knowledge we already possess. This is why when a young person makes a sweeping statement about, say, a heated political issue, we adults tend to say, "It's not as simple as that." The young person doesn't have the breadth of knowledge that an adult does, and therefore his judgments are limited.

Now, what does any of this have to do with faith?

Faith is a way of knowledge. It begins when we trust another person and accept what he says to be true. But this acceptance does not end our relationship with this new bit of information. The new knowledge does not sit in the mind, undisturbed, as water in a glass. The mind immediately goes to work. It begins thinking over the new information—but only if you or I *choose* to put the mind to work.

We must always remember that we have a choice in the matter. We can choose to think, and we can choose to ignore. The choice *is* ours. The freedom *is* ours. Therefore, we are responsible for our own understanding of the knowledge we receive through faith.

So: when the Son of Man returns, will he find faith on the earth? That very much depends on whether we've chosen not only to hear him, but to *listen* to him. Do we merely let his words enter into our minds and sit there, undisturbed? Or do we make the entirely free choice to think about them?

Now, it might come as a surprise to some of us that thinking about the knowledge we obtain by faith is an essential part of Christian spirituality. And this is not a teaching found only in the writings of popes and theologians. It's found in the teaching of Jesus himself.

Let us try to see anew a parable that has become so familiar to us that we hardly see it at all—the Parable of the Sower:

A sower went out to sow. And as he sowed, some seeds fell along the path, and the birds came and devoured them. Other seeds fell on rocky ground, where they had not much soil, and immediately they sprang up, since they had no depth of soil, but when the sun rose they were scorched; and since they had no root they withered away. Other seeds fell upon thorns, and the thorns grew up and choked them. Other seeds fell on good soil and brought forth grain, some a hundredfold, some sixty, some thirty. (Matthew 13:3–8)

Now, we all know that the Lord was not interested in telling us about the farming habits of one particular sower. Rather, we know that the parable is a metaphor that points us to a greater truth. What truth? Apparently, the disciples had the same question, for they approached the Lord later in the day and asked him to explain its meaning. Here's how he responded:

Hear then the parable of the sower. When any one hears the word of the kingdom and does not understand it, the evil one comes and snatches away what is sown in his heart; this is what was sown along the path. As for what was sown on rocky ground, this is he who hears the word and immediately receives it with joy; yet he has no root in himself, but endures for a while, and when tribulation or persecution arises on account of the word, immediately he falls away. As for what was sown among thorns, this is he who hears the word, but the cares of the world and the delight in riches choke the word, and it proves unfruitful. As for what was sown on good soil, this is he who hears the word and understands it; he indeed bears fruit, and yields, in one case a hundredfold, in another sixty, and in another thirty. (Matthew 13:18–32)

What are we being told? That the four types of soil represent four types of souls. Of the four, we tend to focus on the middle two—those who reject the Word for fear of persecution or for love of the world. But, really, it's the fourth type that should interest us, for it's the fourth type that bears fruit. What does this soul do that is different from the other three? What does it do that causes it to blossom?

Let us reread what our Lord says, and this time I'll emphasize his point: "As for what was sown on good soil, this is he who hears the word *and understands it.*" Startling, isn't it? The one who bears fruit—and as much as a hundredfold!—is the one who not only hears the Word, but understands it.

Now, let's contrast the fourth soul with the first. Jesus says: "When any one hears the word of the kingdom and *does not* understand it, the evil one comes and snatches away what is sown in his heart." Again, startling. Our Lord is telling us that we can reject his Word by choosing *not* to understand it, by choosing *not* to think about it.

So: what is the nature of faith? Faith is a way of truth. To believe means to accept what another says to be true and real. *And*—we are able to accept what is said only when we choose to think upon it, to ponder it, to understand it. This is how we make it our own.

What is the role of reason in the way of faith?

We've already touched upon the answer in the previous question. Reason lies between hearing what is spoken and accepting it as true. We cannot accept what we do not understand, and we need reason to understand what we hear. This is why the definition of theology has always been "faith seeking understanding." We hear what the Lord has said, and then we reflect on it, ponder it in our own hearts, striving to understand the mystery of God and our own relationship with him.

But for the Church, reason's role is not limited to understanding what God has told us—though this is an incredible dignity given to our meager human intellects. There are two other ways reason intersects with and relates to faith.

First, we can use reason to help show that the truths of faith are not contrary to the truths we know by reason alone. How many times have we heard that the opening chapters of Genesis have been disproved by science? How many times have we been told that it's illogical to believe that Jesus is God? How many times have we wondered how *one* God can be *three* persons when it's obvious that three does not equal one? We do not have the space to get into such considerations here, but there are answers to these questions—answers that *can* satisfy the human mind, answers that do show that faith and reason are not contrary to one another. We are able to make these arguments because we can use reason to explain why and how these statements of faith do not contradict reason.

Second, and what's most important to this book, we can use reason to demonstrate that it's logical to believe in God, in Christ, and in the Church. Using technical theological jargon, we can use reason to establish the "preambles of faith"—that is, the main, rational grounds for our faith.

There are three main "preambles" of faith, three main rational premises upon which our faith is built. They are:

1. The existence of God.
2. God's authority and right to be believed.
3. That God's self-revelation is confirmed by miracles—primarily the resurrection of Christ.

In each case, we can build a rational argument as to why it's logical and sane to believe that God exists, that we should have faith in him, and that he has revealed himself in Jesus of Nazareth. And that's precisely what this book is about—the preambles of faith (see Hardon, *Modern Catholic Dictionary*, p. 432).

In Chapter 2, we'll focus on proving that God exists. In Chapter 3, we'll establish the rational grounds for believing that Jesus of Nazareth rose from the dead. In Chapter 4, we'll explain why it's rational to believe in the Catholic Church. Now, that the Catholic Church is the one, true Church established by Christ is *not* a preamble of faith in the technical sense of the word, but explaining the rational grounds for being a Catholic rounds out the discussion. How so? Because once we say that God has revealed himself in Christ, the natural question is this one: Where do we find the teachings of Christ today?

And so, the basic outline of this book can be summarized in these three questions:

1. Does God exist?
2. Has he revealed himself in Jesus of Nazareth?
3. Is his revelation found in the Catholic Church?

All right. But why is it important to know the preambles of faith? Why these three questions?

If you're a believing Catholic, you know we live in difficult times—times that challenge the simple faith Catholics have enjoyed in ages past.

At one point, America could be called a "Christian nation." To believe in God was a hallmark of American culture. Prayer was part of school, and on Sundays, only gas stations were open for business. It wasn't only permissible—rather, it was expected—to wish someone Merry Christmas. To proclaim that one believed in God wasn't a mark of defiance. How times have changed! Our culture is no longer a Christian culture, the very existence of God is called into question, and it's become impossible to even mention God in the context of law and morality without inviting scorn on yourself.

And then there's the matter of Christ. For the past several hundred years, liberal Protestant biblical scholars have deconstructed the New Testament, have called into question the reliability of the Gospels, and have taught that the "historical Jesus" is very different from the "Christ of faith." Simply stated, they denied the divinity of Jesus. What was once a debate among Protestant biblical scholars has today become a dominant view within biblical scholarship—a view promoted by the mainstream media. And, unfortunately, this view has snaked its way into the Church, into parish-level catechesis, which tends to over-emphasize the humanity of Jesus at the expense of his divinity. The end result has been a complete dismantling of Catholic devotion: if Jesus is not God, then the Eucharist is only a symbol, nothing more, and the Blessed Mother isn't so blessed after all, since her son is a mere man.

But once you profess that you believe in the full divinity and humanity of Jesus, another question comes our way: "Why are you Catholic?" This question could come from many different viewpoints, but to keep things simple, let's assume it's coming from a Protestant viewpoint. So, when a Protestant asks, "Why are you Catholic?", they are wondering why we subject ourselves to rules coming from Rome and so many "unbiblical" teachings and traditions. "Isn't believing in Jesus enough?" they ask. "Isn't the Bible enough?" Or, if they're more aggressive, they may assert, "Catholicism is anti-Christian. The Pope is the Antichrist. The Catholic Church is the Whore of Babylon." Knowing how to answer these attacks is an important element of understanding our Catholic faith.

Finally, any Catholic who dares reflect seriously on his or her own Catholic faith will ask, "Why do I believe in God … in Christ … in the Church?" It cannot be helped. We are children of our culture, and our culture has rejected God, Christ, and the Church. And the hard, cold fact is that this crisis of faith that is plaguing our culture and, in turn, plaguing the Church, is only just beginning.

And so, when the Son of Man returns, will he find faith on the earth? Yes, he will—but only in those who possess a realized faith. What is a realized faith? Father John Hardon says it's "a well-grounded conviction that what I believe makes sense, that it is not a mirage, that I have reasons for being a Christian and a Catholic, which satisfy my mind as credible" (*Advanced Catholic Catechism Course*, p. 20).

A realized faith is the rock-solid foundation of belief we should all be seeking.

You convinced me—I want a realized faith! What must I do?

Two things. First and foremost, you must pray. Prayer gives you the experiential knowledge that we all desperately seek. Pray for a strong faith. Pray to know Christ better. Pray for wisdom, understanding, and knowledge. Attend Mass often and receive the Eucharist. Go to confession at least once a month, for pureness of life is also a way of knowledge. Meditate on the Gospels and pray the rosary, for the Gospels and the rosary are the best way to contemplate the face of Christ.

Second, you must study. Saint Josemaría Escrivá says that "reading has made many saints" and "an hour of study, for a modern apostle, is an hour of prayer (*The Way*, nos. 116, 335). A century ago, reading and study were not as important as they are today. Today, we have an almost unlimited stream of information coming at us that offer ways of thinking and worldviews that are contrary to Catholic thought. Unless we take an active role in our intellectual formation, we *will* be led astray. Slowly, perhaps. But surely.

How should you study? You need to be committed to developing what Pope John Paul II calls a "deeper and more systematic knowledge of the person and the message of our Lord Jesus Christ" (*On Catechesis in Our Time*, no. 19). This knowledge begins with knowing *why* you believe in God, *why* you believe in Christ, and *why* you believe in the teaching authority of the Church. See these three topics as the three legs of a stool. If any one of them is weak, your stool will be wobbly, and the weaker any of the three are, the more in danger your stool is of collapsing altogether.

Once you grasp the rationale for believing in God, in Christ, and in the Church, you will be able to continue down the road of study with rock-solid confidence. You'll have good reasons for knowing that God exists, that he revealed himself in Jesus of Nazareth, and that his revelation subsists fully in the Catholic Church.

Armed with this confidence, you will have the assurance that the Church does not teach "Catholic" things, but truth itself.

2

WHY WE BELIEVE IN GOD

You said faith means trusting the word of another. But today, when people say, "I believe in God," they mean they believe God exists. Isn't this a contradiction?

Let's make a distinction between "human faith" and "divine faith." Human faith is the faith we give to another human being, and divine faith is that which we give to God.

Everything we've said about human faith can be said about divine faith. To have faith in God means that we trust him and accept what he says as true and real. But there is an extra dimension to divine faith. It takes an added ingredient to trust God. It's this—we must accept that he exists.

Obviously, this element is not part of human faith. When I say I believe in my wife, you do not take me to mean that I believe she exists. If I were to pass on some medical advice I received from my doctor, you would assume, without question, that I was talking about a real flesh-and-blood physician.

The phrase "flesh-and-blood" pinpoints the problem with divine faith. My wife and my doctor—as well as every other human being in whom I believe—have one thing in common: they are tangible realities. But God is invisible. He is beyond the material world. He is unseen. This means that our relationship with God is also invisible, beyond the material world, and unseen. Yes, there are the sacraments, which are physical realities, but they communicate *invisible* grace to us. So what does it mean to have faith in a God we cannot see? At this point, the biblical definition of faith helps us greatly: "Faith is ... the conviction of things not seen" (Hebrews 11:1). Because God is unseen, it takes an act of faith to know he exists, an act of faith to know that he is at work in our lives.

But isn't faith trusting another and accepting his word as true? It is, and that's a good definition—so long as we are speaking only of our interactions with other humans. But we've moved beyond this realm of existence; we've entered a new realm. We are no longer talking about things visible; we are now talking about things invisible. And this difference matters. This is why we walk by faith and not by sight—for the foundation on which all Christian faith rests is an invisible God who transcends the material world.

Therefore, we should think of divine faith as having two elements: first, it means that we believe the unseen God exists, and second, it means that we trust him and accept his word as true and real.

Wait a minute. In the last chapter, you said it's rational to believe that God exists. Now you're saying it's a matter of faith. Explain yourself.

Before I can explain how we know God exists through both faith and reason, I first need to clarify a misconception.

You're assuming that faith and reason are opposed. They're not. Let's recall what John Paul II said: "Faith and reason are like two wings on which the human spirit rises to the truth." They work together: faith allows us to accept as truth what we cannot know through observation and experience, and reason provides the groundwork that makes our faith strong. Perhaps an example will help.

In his little book on faith, the Catholic German philosopher Josef Pieper sets up a situation that illustrates how faith and reason work: "Let us assume that I receive a visit from a stranger who says that he has just returned home from many years as a prisoner of war and tells me that he has seen my brother in prison camp; that this brother, missing for so long and believed to be dead, will probably soon be repatriated" (*Faith, Hope, Love*, p. 27). Now, here's the question: how I might go about trusting this man and accepting his word as true and real?

In other words, how can I believe my brother is alive? That is my desire—for my brother to be alive. But to believe this stranger without any kind of investigation would be sheer folly. So, how do I establish reasons for believing him? First, I can ask him about my brother, and insofar as his answers align with my knowledge of my brother, my reason to trust him is strengthened. Next, there is my own ability to judge his character, an ability based on years of experience meeting new people. Finally, I can visit military officials who can vouch for him. Taken together, I will have solid reasons for trusting the stranger and believing his word. I will have foundations for my faith. I can say from the depths of my heart, My brother is alive! But in the end, until I see my brother for myself, my knowledge that he is alive is based on faith—a faith backed by reason, yes, but it is still faith.

So: whatever truth we acquire through faith, there will always be reasons for our belief. Those reasons provide a solid foundation, and they can give us peace of mind, for we can know that what we know by faith is credible.

Now, we know God exists through faith, but that does not mean we lack reasons for believing. To believe the stranger, I must have reasons to believe him, reasons that provide the foundations for my faith. Something similar is happening with our faith in God. To believe God exists, we must have reasons to believe he exists, and these reasons must be well-grounded and credible.

We should note that the Catholic Church herself recognizes our need to have rational ground for believing that God exists. As Pope John Paul II explains, "This knowledge of God through reason ... is in keeping with man's rational nature. It is in keeping also with the original plan of God, who by endowing man with this nature intends that man be able to know him" (*God, Father and Creator*, p. 43). In other words, God gave us a rational intellect so that we might know him, and when we strive to know God through reason, we are using our intellect as God intends.

To use our intellect in this way is important. Just as we cannot believe our brother is alive until we have reasons for trusting the stranger, we cannot believe what God has said until we are certain he exists. Simply put, we need continuity between what we know by faith and what we know by reason.

So: how do we know God through reason? As the *Catechism of the Catholic Church* says, "God ... can be known with certainty from the created world by the natural light of human reason" (no. 36). And as John Paul II teaches, "God, who through the Word creates all things and keeps them in existence, gives men an enduring witness to himself in created things. This witness is given as a gift and at the same time is left as an object for study on the part of human reason. Through the careful and persevering reading of the witness of created things, human reason is directed toward God and approaches him" (*God, Father and Creator,* p. 43). In other words, we know God through creation.

Throughout the centuries, several theologians have offered "proofs" of God's existence. But these aren't mathematical or scientific proofs. Rather, they prove that it's logical, based on what we can observe in creation, to believe that an all-powerful, all-loving God exists. The most famous proofs come from Saint Thomas Aquinas (1224–1274), whom the Church often looks to as a guide on this matter.

But before we get into these proofs, let's consider the practical side of what we're saying. There should be moments in our spiritual lives when we allow creation to witness to the glory of God. Sometimes this happens unexpectedly; the ocean often reminds me of the immensity of God and my own smallness. But we should also carve out specific ways in which we can use creation as a source of meditation. For example, Saint Ignatius of Loyola (1491–1556) often began his time of prayer gazing at the sky while saying the "Our Father." It's said that he often ended this brief moment with tears in his eyes.

All that we study will have little effect on our lives if we do not elevate it with prayer and meditation. Our reflections on God are not reflections on some abstract reality, but on a personal God who calls us to himself. He doesn't call us because he needs us, but because we need him. Saint Irenaeus (d. 202) says that "the glory of God is man fully alive," but we are only fully alive when we have a personal relationship with God. The clay of this relationship is study, and it receives life from deep and continuous prayer.

Doesn't Sacred Scripture tell us that we can know God's existence through creation?

Yes, it does. Both the Church—and Saint Thomas Aquinas for that matter—follow the teaching of Scripture. Both cite a passage from Romans, which reads, "Ever since the creation of the world [God's] invisible nature, namely, his eternal power and deity, has been clearly perceived in the things that have been made" (Romans 1:20). Thus, the Bible itself teaches that God can be known by creation, and this biblical teaching informed both Church doctrine and Saint Thomas's theology.

For the sake of rounding out our knowledge, let's dig

a little deeper into Sacred Scripture. The biblical teaching is much richer than this one verse suggests. Let's begin by looking at this passage from Romans in its larger context:

> For the wrath of God is revealed from heaven against all ungodliness and wickedness of men who by their wickedness suppress the truth. For what can be known about God is plain to them, because God has shown it to them. Ever since the creation of the world his invisible nature, namely, his eternal power and deity, has been clearly perceived in the things that have been made. So they are without excuse; for although they knew God they did not honor him as God or give thanks to him, but they became futile in their thinking and their senseless minds were darkened. Claiming to be wise, they became fools, and exchanged the glory of the immortal God for images resembling mortal man or birds or animals or reptiles. (Romans 1:18–23)

Saint Paul cannot be clearer: since the beginning of the world, God has revealed his existence through creation. This revelation is so obvious that it can be "clearly perceived in the things that have been made." No one can stand before the majesty of creation and balk at God's existence, and because of the greatness of creation, no one can claim they didn't have the ability to know God, or that they were unable to find him. As John Paul II observes, "The invisible God becomes in a certain way recognized through the things he has made" (*God, Father and Creator*, p. 38).

This truth, which Saint Paul makes so clear, is also found in other biblical passages. Let's focus on just two more. First, let's consider the opening of Psalm 19:

> The heavens are telling the glory
>   of God;
> and the firmament proclaims his
>   handiwork.
> Day to day pours forth speech,
> and night to night declares
>   knowledge.
> There is no speech, nor are there
>   words;
> their voice is not heard;
> yet their voice goes out through all
>   the earth,
> and their words to the end of
>   the world.

The glory of God is revealed across the sky, is revealed day and night. The sun and moon use neither physical words nor human speech, but the truth of God's glory fills the earth, to the end of the world. How is this possible? Because the sun, moon, and stars show forth God's eternal power and divine nature for all to see, at all times of the day and the night. If we do not see God's glory in the heavens, that is our problem. We should pray for the eyes to see correctly.

And then there is the much more important passage from the Book of Wisdom, which is found in the Old Testament:

> For all men who were ignorant of God were foolish by nature; and they were unable from the good things that are seen to know him who exists, nor did they recognize the craftsman while paying heed to his works ... if through delight in the beauty of these things men assumed them to be gods, let them know how much better than these is their Lord, for the author of beauty created them. And if men were amazed at their power and working, let them perceive from them how much more powerful is he who formed them. For from the greatness and beauty of created things comes a corresponding perception of their Creator. (Wisdom 13:1–5)

In fact, the entire passage, which runs another four verses, deserves to be read, reread, and meditated upon. It's that rich. The heart of its meaning is this: we can know the beautiful God through the beauty of creation, but because of sin, we are seduced by creation's beauty. We become so attached to created things that they become like gods to us and we forget our Creator.

At any rate, Scripture is clear: God reveals himself

through creation. Therefore, if we don't recognize that God exists, we are without excuse.

Isn't it easy to dismiss these passages? After all, there are no idols today.

Are you sure about that? Although it's true that most people do not worship images resembling "mortal man or birds or animals or reptiles," that does not mean that the temptation to put creatures before the Creator is eliminated. How many people have claimed Sunday as "me-time" instead of "God-time"? How many people have stopped worshipping God on Sundays in order to get ahead at work, shop, play golf, or simply sleep a little later than normal? How many people don't have time to pray but somehow find the time to watch television? How many people spend hours reading popular fiction or self-help books but never open the Gospels? It's all a matter of values. As Jesus said, "Where your treasure is, there will your heart be" (Matthew 6:21). We spend time on what we value, and we don't waste time on what we don't value. When we stop giving real quality time to God, we can be sure that we value some created thing more than God.

As Archbishop Charles J. Chaput notes,

A central fact of modern American life is idolatry.

Which sounds outlandish. But check the evidence.

We're a nation held together by respect for the law. The seminal law in our civilization comes from the experience of Moses on Mount Sinai.... Until recent decades the Ten Commandments were so widely memorized and revered that almost any citizen could recite them by rote. [...]. The first three speak to our relationship with God. [...]. The God of Israel does not mince words:

1. I am the Lord your God; you shall not place foreign gods before me.

2. You shall not take the name of the Lord your God in vain.

3. Remember to keep holy the Sabbath.

Now here's a simple test. How many public figures, or even personal friends, do you know who genuinely place God first in their thinking? How much of God do you find in American public life? How many times a day are the words "Jesus Christ" abused at work, on the street, in our public entertainment? How many malls close, how many people take a break from work, and how many families disconnect from media, sports, and shopping in order to spend time together, without distractions, on an average Sunday? And how much time do any of us make for silence—the kind of silence that allows God to speak, and us to listen?

For most of us, the answers aren't pretty. American life is a river of noise and pressure, a teeming mass of consumer appetites. It's profoundly ordered *away* from the first three commandments, even when we pay them lip service. (*Strangers in a Strange Land*, pp. 72–73)

But even if you attend Mass on Sundays and pray daily, do not be deceived—the temptation to put creatures before God remains. The same Saint Ignatius who opened his prayer while gazing skyward also wrote a book of meditations called the *Spiritual Exercises*. He used it to lead people—particularly members of the Society of Jesus—deep into the life of prayer. The very first meditation is entitled "The Principle and the Foundation," and it's a meditation on the proper use of created things. Ignatius writes:

> Man is created to praise, reverence, and serve God our Lord, and by this means to save his soul. The other things on the face of the earth are created for man to help him in attaining the end for which he is created. Hence, man is to make use of them in as far as they help him in the attainment of his end, and he must rid himself of them in as far as they prove a hindrance to him. (*Exercises*, no. 23)

What is Saint Ignatius telling us? That when we make an examination of conscience, we need to ask serious questions about the created things in our lives. How do they affect us? Do they help us love God more, or do they keep us from God? If they are helping us love God, we are using them properly. But if they are keeping us from God, why do we keep them around? If something was hurting us physically, we would remove it—quickly! Why don't we remove things that spiritually harm us? Because we don't value our spiritual lives as much as we do our physical lives.

So while we may not be kneeling before a statue of Baal or Osiris, it does not mean we are free from a sinful attachment to created things. Part of our spiritual journey is to become detached from *all* created things, even from the one created thing we love best—our very selves.

Point made, but let's talk about Aquinas. How exactly do we prove—from reason—that God exists? Can we go through Aquinas's five proofs?

I'm hesitant to go through all five of Thomas's proofs. They require a good amount of philosophical background to be fully appreciated. A better idea, I think, would be to get deep into one proof and really try to understand it. For my money, the best proof of God's existence is Thomas's second one—the proof from causality.

If you're new to this kind of thinking, your first steps will be difficult. I suggest you read slowly and strive to make what I say your own. That is the best advice I can give: to make this knowledge your own.

Thomas's proof from causality is rooted in the law of cause and effect. This law has two pillars. First, it states that *every effect must have a cause.* A painting is an effect; it is caused by an artist. The ripples on the lake are effects; they are caused by the wind. Warmth is an effect; it's caused by fire. So far, so good. This is all very basic.

What's also very basic, but perhaps not as obvious, is the second pillar: *every cause is also an effect.* The artist caused the painting. But what caused the artist? The wind caused the ripples. But what caused the wind? The fire caused the warmth. But what caused the fire?

We are simply shifting our focus backward. First, we saw the artist, wind, and fire as causes. We now see them as effects. As are effects, they have their own causes. The artist was caused by his parents. The wind by changes in atmospheric pressure. Fire by chemical combustion.

If we shift our focus backward once again, our new group of causes now become effects. For example, the artist's parents are effects of their own parents.

And we can keep shifting our focus backward. We can keep seeing causes as effects. We can keep doing this until it becomes too staggering to consider.

How do these two principles "prove" or "demonstrate" God's existence? How do they show that it is rational to believe God exists?

Step #1: We observe the world around us and we see that everything is an effect. The clouds are effects of condensation. Houses are effects of builders. Each human being is the effect of his parents.

Step #2: As we ponder what we observe, we see that every cause is also an effect. Trees are caused by sun, seed, and soil. But sun, seed, and soil are also effects. They have their own causes.

Step #3: As we think about the cause and effect relationship, we see that the chain of cause and effect can go backward indefinitely. But herein lies the problem: there cannot be a never-ending chain of cause and effects. To use the language of Saint Thomas, there cannot be an "infinite regression of causes." Consider the following example: the tree is caused by the seed, the seed is caused by the tree, the tree is caused by the seed, the seed is caused by the tree, the tree is caused by the seed, and so on, and so on, and so on.... At some point, this chain of cause-and-effect *must* come to an end. There must be a first tree (or seed) before all other trees (or seeds). If not, there would be no trees and seeds at all.

The conclusion: If every effect is a cause—and if there cannot be a never-ending chain of cause-and-effect —there must be a cause that is not an effect. There must be a *first cause* that stands outside of the cycle of causes-and-effects and sets the cycle in motion. And because this first cause is first—because it stands outside the cycle of cause-and-effect—it is *not* an effect. It is the unaffected cause, that is, the *uncaused cause*. And so, as Saint Thomas concludes, "Therefore it is necessary to admit a first cause, to which everyone gives the name of God."

If this is the first time you've thought along these lines, this is all very difficult. Step Three will be the hardest part of Thomas's argument to grasp. To explain why a "regression into infinity" is impossible would require an incredible amount of philosophy. But since a picture is worth a thousand words, why not illustrate the logic?

I first came across this illustration in Father James Martin's book, *My Life with the Saints* (pp. 265–66), and I've used it with both high-school students and adult students. I have them stand in a circle, then give them two instructions: they are to tap the shoulder of the person standing to their right, but only *after* their own shoulder has been tapped. Then I tell them to begin. After a second or two, they realize I have set up an impossible situation: standing as they are in a circle, they form a self-contained unit, and they are unable to begin the tapping sequence. As they look at me for further instruction, I tap someone on the shoulder—and the tapping begins! Because I stand outside their circle, I'm able to set their tapping in motion. I am the first tapper, the untapped tapper, the one who can tap without having to have been tapped first.

The circle of students is a metaphor for the universe. Despite its vastness and incredible complexity, it *is* a self-contained series of causes-and-effects. For it to have a beginning, there must be a cause that stands outside of it—a cause that was the first cause of every effect, a cause that itself is not a cause. Therefore, a God who is the creator of all things must exist.

Now sometimes, after demonstrating why it's logical to believe there is a first cause of all things, someone will ask, "But who caused God?" While this may be a natural question to ask, it's as illogical as asking if God could make a four-sided triangle. If God is the *first* cause of all things, then he is *first* in a sequence of causes-and-effect, and since nothing is prior to being *first*, nothing can be the cause of God.

But sometimes this logic slides right past the person who asked the question. When this happens, I jump on their train of thought and enjoy the ride. "Okay," I say, "let's suppose something caused God. Let's call the God who created our universe 'God #1,' and let's call the God who created God #1 'God #2.' Now, let me ask you: who created God #2?"

Usually, when I turn the faulty logic back on the one who asked the question, he understands his mistake. If God #1 has a cause, then so does God #2, God #3, God #4, and so on. We must accept that the chain of cause-and-effect cannot regress into infinity. We must realize that not everything can be receivers of existence. We must conclude there is a primary giver of existence who, himself, exists by his own power. At some point, we must accept that there is a *first cause* of all things.

Therefore, as Saint Thomas would say, God exists.

So God exists, but that doesn't mean Christianity is true. How do you connect the two?

You're right: the existence of God does not necessitate the truth of Christianity. We have demonstrated it's logical to believe God exists, but we still need to make a connection between the God we know from reason to the God who revealed himself in Jesus Christ. We need to show the link between God and Christianity.

To do this, let's return to the three questions that provide the outline of this book:

1. Does God exist?
2. Has God revealed himself?
3. Is God's revelation found in the Catholic Church?

Now, for the sake of clarity, let's draw a line between Question 1 and Question 2. This means that we see Question 1 as something of a stand-alone question, and we're pairing Questions 2 and 3.

Why are we doing this?

Because God's existence really does stand apart from whether God has revealed himself and whether this revelation is found in Catholic Church. More to the point, one cannot speak abstractly about God's revelation. If God has spoken, he has spoken to a certain person who lived at a certain period of time—which means we can point to a time and place in which God has spoken. Going forward, we need to build a bridge between the God we know through reason to the God who has revealed himself in human history to a human person.

So, how do we build this bridge from the God of reason to the God of revelation? How do we move from God's existence to the truth of Christianity?

Here's how I see it. Imagine a chasm. On one side is God, and on the other are the five great religions of the world: Buddhism, Christianity, Hinduism, Islam, and Judaism. Our goal is to build a bridge across this chasm and connect God to one of these religions.

Why am I limiting myself to these five religions? Someone might object that by not taking into consideration every religion of the world that I'm stacking the deck in favor of Christianity. But that's not true. If we can show that God has *not* revealed himself to one of these five, we can look elsewhere, at the many forms of African paganism, for example, or Shintoism, or Zoroastrianism, or the Native American religions. But to try to survey every religion of the world would be futile. Instead of stacking the deck in favor of Christianity, we would be stacking the deck in favor of exhaustion. It only seems logical to begin with the "Big Five," so to speak.

Someone else may object that I've lumped the many varieties and flavors of Buddhism, Christianity, Hinduism, Islam, and Judaism into five homogeneous groups that do not exist in the real world. A similar reason as above applies here. At this point, it does not make sense to think about the divisions within, say, Christianity. Tell me what the differences between Baptists and Mormons matter if Christianity itself can be proven wrong. So let's first try to figure out which religion possesses God's revealed truth—if, in fact, God has revealed himself.

Now, as we look at the five great religions, we cannot forget what we have already learned—namely, that from creation and through the light of reason we know that God exists. If we think a little deeper about what it means for God to be both the *first* cause and the *uncaused* cause, we will see that there can be only *one* God, for if there were more than one God, then the actions of one god would affect the other god. Once we say that these gods can be affected, they would become receivers of existence, not pure existence, and we would be back to our first question —what caused these gods? Thus, there is only one God.

If there is only one God—and if this God stands wholly outside the material world as its creator—we can rule out Buddhism and Hinduism. Buddhism not only lacks a worked-out theology of God, it lacks any clear idea of God. This is the reason it's so popular today: it's a religion without God. And with its millions of gods, Hinduism is fully polytheistic, without a trace of monotheism in its DNA.

Having eliminated two, we are now down to three: Christianity, Islam, and Judaism. Immediately, our path becomes more difficult. How so? Each is monotheistic. Each believes God has revealed himself. Each believes that it is the one, true religion established by the one, true God. And each claims Abraham to be its ancient father of faith. We are at something of a deadlock, and nothing we have learned about the God of creation can break it. The only way forward is by shifting our focus. We must now look at the claims made by Christianity, Islam, and Judaism.

But how should we go about our task at hand? Looking at specific doctrines won't offer much help. The very nature of religious doctrine is that it is peculiar to the religion that teaches it. Comparing doctrines leads us nowhere. Christianity says God is three persons in one nature, but Islam and Judaism say that God is only one person. Okay. We've successfully compared these religions, but we haven't answered the question about which one is correct. Moral teachings won't do us any good, either. Moral principles can be known by reason, which means the basic commands we find in Christianity, Islam, and Judaism we will also find in ancient Babylonian, Egyptian, and Norse religions as well as the writings of the ancient Greek, Roman, and

Chinese thinkers. So: how do we break through this deadlock?

Let's go back to Romans. Saint Paul writes, "Ever since the creation of the world [God's] invisible nature, namely, his eternal power and deity, has been clearly perceived in the things that have been made" (Romans 1:20). But why would God make himself known through creation *unless* he wanted us to know him? Wanting us to know him, he created all things to be signs of his existence. Now, if God has revealed himself to us in a special way, would he not provide a sign of this revelation? Would not this sign be clearly perceived? Would it not point to the time and place of his revelation?

I cannot see how the answers to these questions can be "no." If God has revealed himself, he has revealed himself *for a reason,* and the most obvious of all reasons is that *he wants us to know what he has to say.* Therefore, there must be *something* within one of these religions that is a sign that God has revealed himself. But what?

As noted, this sign cannot be a particular doctrine. Doctrines are specific to a religion. You prove a doctrine by proving the veracity of the religion that teaches it. Whatever sign God has given must stand outside of Christianity, Islam, or Judaism itself; it must come prior to the religion. And the only thing that is prior to Christianity, Islam, or Judaism is the act of God's revelation— which focuses on a time, a place, and a person. Of these three, time and place are insignificant. Three men standing in the same place at the same time can all claim that God has revealed himself. The only thing that is different are the men. This means the sign that points to God's revelation must lie in the person who founded the religion. This means our focus is no longer on Christianity, Islam, and Judaism, but, rather, on Jesus, Mohammed, and Moses.

Of these three, is there one who stands apart, who is completely unlike the other two? There is. It's Jesus of Nazareth. And what makes him so very different from the other two is this: *his followers claim he rose from the dead.*

If he truly rose from the dead, this event would be the surefire sign that God revealed himself in Jesus of Nazareth. It would be the surefire sign that Christianity is the one, true religion established by the one, true teacher of God's revealed truth.

This means that the resurrection of Jesus is the bridge the crosses the chasm! If we can prove that Jesus rose from the dead, we can answer "yes" to our second and third questions: we can prove that God has revealed himself, and we can prove that his revelation is found in the Catholic Church. Right?

Almost. Just because we can prove that Jesus rose from the dead does *not* mean that Catholicism is the one, true religion. That's why, above, I said that Jesus's resurrection would be the surefire sign that *Christianity* was the one, true religion. We still would have to demonstrate why it's logical to believe that Christ founded the Catholic Church.

But you're on the right track. We know why it's logical to believe that God exists. Now it's time to show why it's logical to believe that Jesus rose from the dead.

3

WHY WE BELIEVE IN JESUS OF NAZARETH

Before we look at Jesus's resurrection, I have a question. I've heard that we can't be sure that Jesus ever lived. How do you respond to a claim like that?

If anyone is going to doubt that Jesus existed, they must also doubt that Plato existed, or Julius Caesar existed, or Charlemagne existed—or any other historical figure that predates the photograph. And given how we can manipulate photographs today, who knows, maybe Abraham Lincoln didn't exist, either. Either we accept history as a valid source of knowledge, or we don't. If we accept it as valid, then we must accept *all* of it as valid. We can't pick and choose which facts we want to believe and which ones we don't. There is no serious historian today who doubts that Jesus of Nazareth actually lived. They may doubt a lot of things Christians say about Jesus, but they don't doubt he was a real, flesh-and-blood human being who lived in first-century Palestine, who was a Jewish religious teacher, and who died at the hands of the Romans.

Simply stated, we can be completely confident Jesus existed, and we should pray for those who deny this basic historical fact.

But some people say that the Gospels are fictions and that there are almost no references to Jesus outside the Gospels. But if Jesus was really as influential as we claim, wouldn't everyone have been writing about him?

One of my favorite words is *anachronistic*. Something is anachronistic when we take an idea from one period of time and apply it to another period of time. For example, as much as I love the movie *Braveheart*, it is highly anachronistic to have a twelfth-century Scotsman cry out: "They may take away our lives, but they'll never take our freedom!" The twentieth-century concept of political freedom would not have made sense to anyone living in the Middle Ages.

In the same way, let's not think that Jesus's influence —if that's really the right word for it—would have extended much beyond the early Christians. Roman culture was the dominant culture at the time, and it was soaked with paganism. At best, Christianity was seen as another religion in a world overflowing with religions; at worst, Christians were despised for their strict moral and strange religious views and, sometimes, arrested and put to death for these views. The massive influence Christ eventually had on the world would not begin until 313, when Emperor Constantine declared Christianity to be the official religion of Rome. And even then, pagan practices continued for decades.

So this idea that Jesus was some incredibly well-known religious figure throughout the Greco-Roman world that historians would have written of is flat out wrong. He *was* incredibly well-known in Jewish circles, particularly those circles that operated in Judea and Galilee, the part of the world where Jesus himself lived and died. That much is true. But no Greek or Roman would have given him much of a second thought. He was nothing but a Jewish rabbi who was executed by the Romans. What's so special about that?

If I sound flippant, it's because I'm trying to make a point: we cannot think that our own modern-day notions of fame and influence were operating in the first century. People were not famous for being famous (think: Paris Hilton). People were not famous for doing stupid things (think: reality TV stars). People were not famous for being insane mass murderers (think: Charles Manson). And people were not famous for being incredibly popular religious teachers (think: Joel Osteen). Who were the famous men of the ancient world? The men who could stamp out a town, a city, or wage war against the Roman Empire. In short, the famous were political and military leaders.

All of this reminds me of something I read by the Anglican bishop Paul Barnett. He wrote a book called *Is the New Testament Reliable?*, and he devotes a few chapters to the extra-biblical evidence for Jesus's existence that we find in ancient historical writings. Bishop Barnett's key point is this: "Had he led a military rebellion against the Romans ... Jesus may have left a greater imprint on [ancient] history. But a harmless Jewish rabbi from a distant minor province accompanied by only twelve followers, who met his death by crucifixion, would not inspire much interest among the writers of that day" (p. 15). Because Jesus didn't do anything that any ancient historian would see as important, we shouldn't expect to find any reference to him in ancient history. And if he never existed, we shouldn't find any at all. The fact that there are even a few references should eliminate any doubt that Jesus of Nazareth really existed.

That is about all we can say here on the matter. If you're really interested in pursuing this topic, I point you toward Bishop Barnett's book.

Now I have a question about the Gospels. How do we respond to someone who says they are fiction?

To respond, we will need to answer two questions. First, who wrote the Gospels? And second, when were they written?

Why these questions? Because, generally speaking, people who doubt the historical accuracy of the Gospels do so for one of two reasons.

First, they claim the Gospels were originally anonymous documents that received the titles *Matthew, Mark, Luke* and *John* sometime in the second century. They argue that these names were chosen in order to link the Gospels to eyewitnesses of Jesus. In other words, this view claims that the Gospels were *not* written by eyewitnesses of the life and death of Jesus, and that the early Church, in order to give authority to the Gospels, had to lie about who wrote them.

Second, people who doubt the historical reliability of the Gospels argue that they were written four, five, and six decades after the death of Jesus. They argue that memories had faded and that myth was mingled with history, that the Gospels are a mix of fact and fiction. Therefore, those serious about studying them must constantly separate truth from fiction, or, as modern scholars like to say, separate the "Jesus of history" from the "Christ of faith."

The conclusion is obvious: if one or both of these scenarios are true, then the Gospels are not historically reliable.

But before we answer these objections, we should take a moment to understand why this issue is so important—to you and me, regular, Mass-attending Catholics with no vested interest in scholarly debates. We must always be on guard against the seeds of doubt, and the evil one has done a masterful job at casting doubt on the Gospels. Our faith in Christ depends on our faith in the Gospels. So let's look at three reasons why this issue is of some importance to us.

First, if the historical reliability of the Gospels can be doubted, so can Christianity. If the Jesus whom Christians worship is the not the same as the Jesus who walked this earth, Christianity is a fool's religion. So what better way to get people to leave the Church than by suggesting the "Christ of faith" is not the same as the "Jesus of history"?

Second, if the historical reliability of the Gospels can be doubted, so can everything Jesus said about the Church and the sacraments. The Catholic claim that Jesus instituted the Church is called into question. Those who say that the Gospels were written four or five decades after the death of Jesus say that every reference to an official church was added to Jesus's original teaching in order to support a hierarchy of leadership. So: did Jesus really make Peter the rock on which he would build his church, or is that just a bill of goods sold by early Christian leaders who were in places of power and did not want to lose them?

And third, if the Gospels are not historically reliable, what does this mean for our relationship with Christ? It means, as Pope Benedict XVI observes, that "intimate friendship with Jesus, on which everything depends, is in danger of clutching at thin air" (*Jesus of Nazareth*, p. xii). If we are to have faith and friendship with Jesus that is so essential to the Christian life, we have no option: we must know why the Gospels are historically reliable.

Wow, I never realized how important this issue was! Let's get down to business. Answer the first question for me—*Who wrote the Gospels?*

You already know who wrote the Gospels—Matthew, Mark, Luke, and John did! But perhaps you've heard otherwise. Perhaps you've heard that these four men did not write the Gospels. Perhaps you've heard that we don't really know who wrote the Gospels, that the Gospels were originally anonymous documents that didn't receive their names until the middle of the second century. So the real challenge before us is this one: how do we defend the traditional view? How do we establish a rock-solid argument for our belief that Matthew, Mark, Luke, and John really wrote the four Gospels?

Let's face it, the mainstream media loves to highlight any and every idea that challenges traditional and orthodox Christianity. This means that our faith in the Gospels is constantly under attack. But more alarming is how the "anonymous Gospel theory" has made its way into parish-level catechesis. It's part of the standard way the Gospels are taught nowadays: one *must* assert that while we don't know who wrote them, we do know that Matthew, Mark, Luke, and John were *not* the original writers.

But perhaps you have never asked these kinds of questions, and perhaps none of this seems all that important to you. Let me assure you—it is! I've dealt with this issue too many times not to know that our faith in Christ *depends* upon showing why it is rational to believe that Matthew, Mark, Luke, and John are indeed the authors of the four Gospels.

So: how do we argue that the anonymous Gospel theory is nonsensical and that the only rational view to hold is that Matthew, Mark, Luke, and John are the authors of the four Gospels? In his book, *The Case for Jesus*, Catholic theologian Brant Pitre shows there are three problems with the anonymous Gospel theory (pp. 12–23). First, no anonymous copies exist. Second, the anonymous scenario is impossible to accept. And third, it would be absurd to give the names *Mark* and *Luke* to two of the Gospels. Let's look at these in order.

(1) NO ANONYMOUS COPIES EXIST

Of all the ancient copies of the Gospels we possess, every one of them begins with one of four titles: "The Gospel according to Matthew," "the Gospel according to Mark," "the Gospel according to Luke," or "the Gospel according to John." But critics claim that the Gospels were written toward the end of the first century and that the names Matthew, Mark, Luke, and John were not given to the Gospels until the middle of the second century. That means that these anonymous documents were being hand-copied and passed around for at least fifty to eighty years before they received a title. One would think we would have found at least one anonymous copy. But we haven't. Every ancient copy we have of the Gospels bears the name of one of the four evangelists. We might argue that once the names were given to the Gospels, Church leaders went back and wrote in the appropriate attribution, but once we look at the second point, we'll see that's an utterly ludicrous idea.

(2) THE ANONYMOUS SCENARIO IS IMPOSSIBLE

In the ancient world, documents were copied by hand, time and again, and were circulated throughout the Roman Empire. The four gospels (as well as the other twenty-three books of the New Testament) were passed from Christian community to Christian community in this way. How many copies of the Gospels existed by the middle of the second century? There is no way to know. We do know they were spread far and wide, from Spain to Italy, throughout Greece and the Middle East, as well throughout North Africa.

The critics of the traditional view of authorship claim that sometime in the middle of the second century the four anonymous Gospels were given names in order to link them to the apostles, so what a miracle that *every* copy of the first Gospel was attributed to Matthew, the second to Mark, the third to Luke, and the fourth to John. What a miracle that the name Mark wasn't accidentally given to the fourth Gospel, or that John wasn't mistakenly given to the first Gospel. And what a miracle that, all throughout the Roman Empire, *only* these four names were used for these four Gospels. What a miracle that no one thought to give the name Phillip to the third Gospel, or the name Andrew to the second.

It seems that the critics who are so eager to dismiss the miracles of Jesus are more than willing to accept a miraculous event far greater than most found in the Bible.

(3) THE GOSPELS OF MARK AND LUKE

There's a final reason to reject the anonymous Gospel theory. It rests upon the authors of the second and third Gospels—Mark and Luke. Who were these men?

Mark may have been an eyewitness of Jesus's life and death, but we don't know for sure. Known as John-Mark, he was a close companion of Saint Peter, with whom he traveled to Rome. And then there's Luke. He was not an eyewitness of Jesus. A Gentile and a physician, he was an early convert to Christianity, and he traveled extensively with Saint Paul. But even though Mark and Luke were associated with Peter and Paul, *neither were apostles.* And neither seemed to be of any importance in the early Church. Then why do we know about them? Because their names are associated with the middle two Gospels.

So: if the Gospels were originally anonymous, and if titles were given to them in the second century—why were the names Mark and Luke selected? If the goal was to give the weight of apostolic authority to the Gospels, would it not seem more logical to select names from Jesus's closest followers? Names of men who were eyewitnesses of his life, death, and resurrection? Names of important men in the apostolic Church? Names of the apostles themselves? Names like Peter, Andrew, or James?

But their names were not chosen. Why not? Perhaps because the names attached to the four Gospels weren't chosen at all. Perhaps because the Gospels were never anonymous documents. Perhaps because from the moment they began being copied, the names of the original authors were attached to them.

Perhaps because Matthew, Mark, Luke, and John are the original writers of the Gospels. If this is true, we have a real reason to believe they are reliable.

Aren't you getting a little ahead of yourself? What about the second question you raised—*When were the Gospels written?* Doesn't the reliability of the Gospels depend on this question, too?

It does! I've heard people say that we can't trust the Gospels because they were written decades after Jesus's death. I've heard people say that the "Jesus of history" isn't the same as the "Christ of faith." I've heard people say that this or that part of the Gospels can't be trusted because forty or more years separated their writing from the actual events, which means memories can fade and fiction can creep into fact. So yes, the reliability of the Gospels depends on *when* they were written.

According to the consensus of modern biblical scholarship, the Gospel of Mark was written first, a little after AD 70. Matthew and Luke came in the 80s, and in that order. Finally, John wrote in the 90s.

But why does modern scholarship claim that no Gospel was written *before* 70? That's the year the Roman general Titus leveled the Jerusalem Temple. Modern scholars focus on this event because Matthew, Mark, and Luke tell us that Jesus prophesied the destruction of the Temple (Matthew 24; Mark 13:1–37; Luke 21:5–36), and many modern scholars have trouble believing that Jesus could have actually done so. Now they have a dilemma. They assume Jesus could not predict the future, but the Gospels show Jesus predicting the future; therefore, they conclude that the Gospels had to have been written *after* the event itself.

The problem with this theory is that modern scholarship assumes bad intention on the part of the Gospel writers. Matthew, Mark, and Luke knew that Jesus never predicted the destruction of the Temple, but they wanted to include it anyway, so they lied about it. They gave him words he never said and an ability he never possessed. Why would they do such a thing? Because, as the theory goes, the "Jesus of history" is not the same as the "Christ of faith." Fiction was mixed with fact, and the Christ who Christians worshipped never really existed.

Of course, could we not assume bad faith on the part of the scholars who first developed and perpetuated this idea? Had they so lost their faith in the divinity of Christ that they assume the Gospel writers *lied* about what Jesus said? Thankfully, some contemporary biblical scholars, both Catholic and Protestant, are now critical of this view.

At any rate, just because we can cast doubt on the view that the Gospels were written four or five decades after Jesus's death does not mean our job is finished. We need to demonstrate that it's logical to accept a much earlier dating of the Gospels of Matthew, Mark, and Luke. (Regarding the Gospel of John, both the traditional view and the modern view are the same: he wrote his Gospel around the year 90.)

To show that a much earlier dating of the Synoptic Gospels is rational, we turn to the end of the Acts of the Apostles. Why Acts of the Apostles? For three reasons.

1. It was written by Luke—the same man who wrote the third Gospel.

2. Acts of the Apostles was Luke's *second* volume. He wrote his Gospel first (Acts 1:1–2).

3. While modern scholars debate whether Matthew or Mark wrote first (the majority hold that Mark did), no one doubts that Luke wrote his Gospel third, after Matthew and Mark had written theirs. In fact, Luke opens his Gospel by telling us that other Gospels had already been written (Luke 1:1–3).

Taken together, these facts tell us that if we can establish when Luke wrote Acts, we can formulate a reasonable theory of when he wrote his Gospel. And if we know when Luke wrote his Gospel, we can make a better guess at when Matthew and Mark wrote theirs. This is why we focus on the end of the Acts of the Apostles, for it ends in a very intriguing way:

> And when we came to Rome, Paul was allowed to stay by himself, with the soldier that guarded him.... And he lived there two whole years at his own expense, and welcomed all who came to him, preaching the kingdom of God and teaching about the Lord Jesus Christ quite openly and unhindered. (Acts 28:16, 30–31)

What are we being told? That Acts of the Apostles ends two years after Paul arrives in Rome, and that Paul is still alive. This begs the question: when did

Paul arrive in Rome? He arrived in AD 60—which means that Luke finished writing Acts in 63, or perhaps a little later, but not too much later, because Paul was beheaded around 65. There can be no doubt that, had he known about it, Luke would have included Paul's martyrdom in the Acts of the Apostles. After all, Paul is one of the book's primary protagonists (the other is Peter), and his martyrdom would have been the perfect ending to Acts of the Apostles—just as it was the perfect ending to a life filled with sufferings for Christ.

What does this mean for the dating of Matthew, Mark, and Luke? If Luke wrote Acts in 63, then he had to have written his Gospel *before* 63. (Note: this is at least a twenty-year difference from the modern view, which holds that Luke wrote sometime in the 80s.) If he wrote his Gospel before 63, the Gospels of Matthew and Mark were also written before 63—much earlier than 63, in fact, for Luke's Gospel was written *third*. In other words, to believe Matthew, Mark, or Luke were written after AD 70 completely dismisses the testimony of the New Testament itself. Rather, it's far more reasonable to assume the first three Gospels were written earlier than 70.

How much earlier? That we cannot know for sure. But consider the dates proposed by the most traditional and conservative Catholic Bible on the market today: the *Douay-Rheims*. The *Douay-Rheims* opens each Gospel with editorial notes that adhere strictly to traditional views of dates and authorship. In these notes we are told the following:

- Matthew wrote about six years after the death, resurrection, and ascension of Christ.
- Mark wrote about ten years after Christ's ascension.
- Luke wrote about twenty-four years after Christ's ascension.

If Christ was crucified in AD 33, this means that Matthew was written around 40, Mark around 43, and Luke around 57—which puts the Gospel of Luke awfully close to the composition of Acts of the Apostles in 63.

Are these dates correct? We cannot know for sure. But what we can be reasonably sure about is that Matthew, Mark, Luke, and John are the authors of the four Gospels; that Matthew, Mark, and Luke were all written before AD 60; and that Matthew and Mark wrote their Gospels several years before Luke did.

Therefore, Matthew, Mark, and Luke were written much closer to Jesus's life and death than what modern scholarship proposes. This means that the possibility of "myth" and "fiction" entering into the Gospels is far less. And if Matthew really did write a mere six years after Christ's ascension, then we can be sure his Gospel would have been read by *other* eyewitnesses of the Lord —including the other apostles themselves. In fact, given the more traditional dates proposed above—dates we look to because of the ending of Acts—the possibility of the Gospels of Matthew, Mark, and Luke being read by other eyewitnesses is quite likely. These other eyewitnesses would have provided a vetting-like process: how could untruth enter the Gospels without being exposed as untruth by people who had seen Jesus with their own eyes, heard him with their own ears, and very likely talked with him, traveled with him, and ate with him? All of this tells us that the entire notion that the truth of the "historical Jesus" has been overshadowed by the mythic "Christ of faith" can be dismissed as, well, a fiction about what really happened.

If we can be sure that Matthew, Mark, Luke, and John are the truth authors of the Gospels—and if we can be sure that Matthew, Mark, and Luke wrote the Gospels one or two decades after Jesus's death— what else is there to discuss in order to prove the Gospels are reliable?

One thing only: we must show that the men who wrote the Gospels are trustworthy. Remember, faith means we trust another person to the point of accepting his word as true and real. In the case of the Gospels, it means having a credible reasons to trust their authors.

This topic can be expanded to the whole of the New Testament. Why? Because the Acts of the Apostles purports to tell us the history of the apostles (especially Peter and Paul), and the rest of the New Testament assumes that the way Jesus is presented in the Gospels is a true and accurate depiction of his life, death, and resurrection. Because the twenty-seven books of the New Testament teach the same truth about Jesus of Nazareth, our faith in Christ rests not only on the four Gospels, but on the *entire* New Testament. So if we want to have a realized faith in New Testament, we need to have reasons to trust its authors so we can believe their words to be true. How do we go about doing so? By looking at the men who wrote the New Testament.

The twenty-seven books of the New Testament were written by eight or nine men. We've already met four of them: Matthew, Mark, Luke, and John. Matthew and John were two of the twelve apostles. Mark was a follower of Jesus, and a close companion of Peter. Luke was a Gentile convert and companion of Paul. These four men gave us nine books of the New Testament: Matthew and Mark each wrote a Gospel; Luke wrote a Gospel and Acts of the Apostles; and John wrote a Gospel, three letters (1, 2, and 3 John) and the Book of Revelation.

Next comes Paul. Neither a follower of Jesus nor one of the twelve, he was an apostle. Why? Because he was called and sent by the risen Jesus himself (Acts 9:1–19). His experience with the risen Jesus influences every word he wrote. He gave us at least thirteen letters of the New Testament: Romans, 1 Corinthians, 2 Corinthians, Galatians, Ephesians, Philippians, Colossians, 1 Thessalonians, 2 Thessalonians, 1 Timothy, 2 Timothy, Titus, and Philemon. He is also the apostolic and eyewitness authority behind the Gospel of Luke and the Acts of the Apostles.

Then there is the Letter to the Hebrews. In the early Church, there was some debate as to who wrote Hebrews, but the majority opinion held that Paul was the author. Because of the radically different literary style, Pauline authorship is doubted by most New Testament scholars today. But there are thematic similarities between Hebrews and Paul's letters, so it's reasonable to assume that if Paul didn't write Hebrews then someone very familiar with Paul's theology did (Hahn, *Catholic Bible Dictionary*, 350–51). At any rate, Hebrews is connected to Paul, which is why it's included in the New Testament.

We now move from Hebrews to the Letter of James. Who was James? The answer can be a bit confusing, as there may have been three different Jameses who personally knew Jesus. Two were apostles; if there was a third, he was not. The James who wrote the letter is most likely the brother of the Lord, and he may have been the apostle known as "the Less." Does it make a difference if James the brother of the Lord and James the Less are the same man or were different men? No. For if they were different, then both were eyewitnesses to the life of Jesus Christ—and that is the key point we are trying to make. (See Hahn, *Catholic Bible Dictionary*, 414–15.)

After the Letter of James comes the two letters of Peter. We know who Peter is: not just an apostle, but the leader of the apostles as well as the apostolic authority behind the Gospel of Mark.

After the letters of Peter comes the Letter of Jude. The name "Jude" is short for "Judas," and once again, there is some confusion about how many Judases there were. There is, of course, Judas Iscariot, the betrayer, and it's for this reason that the other Judases (if there are more than one) are known simply as "Jude." But are there one or two Judes? We know there is Jude Thaddaeus, one of the twelve apostles, and we know there is Jude, the author of the Letter of Jude. Now, the author of the letter does not identify himself as an apostle of Christ, but, rather, as "a servant of Jesus Christ and brother of James" (Jude 1:1). An apostle of the Lord is certainly a servant of the Lord, but if he was an apostle, why didn't he just say so? And to which James was he the brother of? We believe he was the brother of the same James who was also the brother of the Lord—which, of course, would make Jude the brother of the Lord as well! In other words, the author of the Letter of Jude was one of Jesus's cousins. But are Jude the Apostle and Jude the writer of the letter the same person? Once again, for what we are trying to accomplish here, it does not matter. For even if they were different men, they still were both eyewitnesses of Jesus, and that is what is most important to us at the moment. (See Hahn,

Catholic Bible Dictionary, 488–89; Sheed, *To Know Christ Jesus*, p. 194.)

After Jude comes the letters of John and the Book of Revelation, of which we have already spoken.

Why did we walk through the authors of the New Testament? Two reasons. First, we need to know that every book of the New Testament is connected to *one of six* eyewitness of the life, death, and resurrection of Jesus of Nazareth. Instead of summarizing all that has been said, this conceptual chart is certainly worth a thousand words:

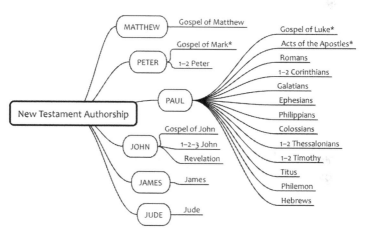

* Written by someone other than the eyewitness authority.

Second, of the six eyewitnesses who are the foundation of the New Testament, we know that at least three of them suffered martyrdom for proclaiming that Jesus rose from the dead. Which three? Matthew, Peter, and Paul. And if James and Jude were also apostles, then that means five of the six eyewitness authorities of the New Testament suffered death for what they said about Jesus.

Does not this prove their trustworthiness?

In a word—yes. Because of their deaths, we should have the utmost confidence to accept what they wrote about Jesus to be true and real.

Let's step back and get our bearings. We're talking about why we believe Jesus rose from the dead. We've shown that he actually existed, and we made a case for why we should trust the Gospels. It's now time to focus on the resurrection, right?

That's right. Logically, we've established that we can trust what the Gospels and the New Testament tell us about Jesus. But there is something else we need to look at before we look at the resurrection itself. We need to remind ourselves why the resurrection is important.

We saw earlier that the resurrection of Jesus is the bridge the connects God's existence with God's revelation. Just because we know God exists doesn't mean he has revealed himself. Or, as we noted above, just because God exists doesn't mean Christianity is true. But if Jesus really rose from the dead, that would be a profound sign that God *had* revealed himself in and through Jesus of Nazareth. It means that the resurrection confirms and ratifies whatever Jesus said and did.

Here, I am reminded of something Bishop Robert Barron said—namely, that "Jesus did not draw his followers' attention primarily to his words," but rather, "he drew it to himself" (*Catholicism*, p. 13). All other great religious and philosophical teachers point away from themselves toward the truth they want to hand on. They say, "I found the way, I found the truth, and I found the life; come, let me show you." Jesus of Nazareth, however, says:

> I am the way, and the truth, and the life; no one comes to the Father, but by me. If you had known me, you would have known my Father also; henceforth you know him and have seen him. (John 14:6–7)

Or consider what he says about the bread of heaven:

> I am the bread which came down from heaven. [...]. Truly, truly, I say to you, unless you eat the flesh of the Son of man and drink his blood, you have no life in you; he who eats my flesh and drinks my blood has eternal life, and I will raise him up at the last day. (John 6:41; 53–54)

Finally, consider what Jesus says about his own teaching:

> Heaven and earth will pass away, but my words will not pass away. (Matthew 24:35)

Who can say such things with a straight face? Who can believe such things? Only a lunatic can utter such words, and only the mentally unstable can believe them … unless the speaker is the Son of God made man in whom we can trust and believe because he has given us a credible reason for our faith—such as rising from the dead.

Also, the resurrection is essential to Christianity itself. It's *the* foundational truth on which Christianity is built. As Saint Paul teaches: "If Christ has not been raised then our preaching is useless and your believing is useless … we are the most unfortunate of all people" (1 Corinthians 15:14, 19; *Jerusalem Bible*). And as Pope Benedict XVI writes, "The Christian faith stands or falls with the truth of the testimony that Christ is risen from the dead" (*Jesus of Nazareth: Holy Week,* p. 241). If there's no rational ground for believing in the resurrection, our faith in Jesus is as strong as tissue paper. If there's no intelligent way we can speak of Jesus's resurrection as a verifiable historical fact, faith in the resurrection becomes a matter of taste, like preferring blue over red, or Mexican food over Italian.

To use the cutting words that Catholic writer Flannery O'Connor used when asked if she believed in the real presence of Christ in the Eucharist, "If it's only a symbol, then to hell with it!" So, too, with Christianity —if the resurrection of Jesus didn't happen.

But if the resurrection of Jesus is that important, why don't the Gospels present a single, unified narrative of the resurrection? When we read them back-to-back, we see contradictions. If they can't agree as to what happened when Jesus was raised from the dead, then how are we supposed to trust them?

The question you have raised is not new. It has been asked many, many times throughout the centuries. Let's provide some answers.

We must remember that eyewitnesses to any event will each have their own version: they will notice different things, remember different details. Just ask a family to describe a recent vacation to Disney World; you'll get different stories, and different versions of the same story. What's true for a family vacation is true for any event. It's particularly true for highly emotional events—and the resurrection of Jesus would have been a highly emotional event for every eyewitness.

Both the women and the apostles had witnessed the trial and horrifying execution of their beloved rabbi. This despair would have been augmented by suddenly finding his tomb empty. The appearance of angels would have done little to ease their minds. And the news of Jesus being raised from the dead would have been more confusing than joyful—at least initially. None of this helps mental clarity. It's safe to assume that the contradictions we find in the Gospels have their origins in the eyewitness testimony themselves.

There is something else to consider. Since when do contradictions disprove an event actually happened? Police officers rarely receive identical stories when they interview witnesses of a car accident, but they do not assume any of the witnesses are lying. In fact, contradictions are expected. The whole point of a police investigation is to see through the apparent contradictions and reconstruct the truth of the event. And the key word is *apparent*. Just because the Gospels *look* like they are contradicting one another does not mean they are.

This is all well and good, but I've read Matthew 28, Mark 16, Luke 24, and John 20—all four resurrection accounts. The most difficult problem has to do with the women who are coming and going from Jesus's tomb. Everything seems to revolve around them. How do you explain these "apparent" contradictions?

About a hundred years ago, a French Catholic theologian named Ferdinand Prat addressed this very question in the second volume of his two-volume work, *Jesus Christ: His Life, His Teaching, and His Work* (pp. 410–36). In it, he addresses the problems associated with the women by asking four questions. (1) Who are they? (2) When did they arrive at the tomb? (3) What did they see, hear, and do? And (4) how did they respond? Borrowing from Father Prat's book, let's answer each.

(1) WHO ARE THE WOMEN?

All four Gospels tell us that Mary Magdalene went to the tomb to finish preparing Jesus's body for burial. But that is about all the Gospels agree upon.

Matthew tells us that Magdalene went with "the other Mary" (Matthew 28:1), but he doesn't tell us who this other Mary was.

Mark provides the answer: "And when the sabbath was past, Mary Magdalene, Mary the mother of James, and Salome brought spices so that they might go anoint him" (Mark 16:1). We now know who the other Mary is; she is the mother of James, the "the brother of the Lord," who was perhaps the apostle known as James the Less. And then there is Salome, who is the wife of Zebedee and mother of James and John, the two brothers called along with Peter and Andrew (Matthew 4:18–22), both of whom were apostles.

Luke, however, tells us that "Mary Magdalene and Joanna and Mary the mother of James" as well as some "other women" went to Jesus's tomb (Luke 24:10). But he does not tell us who these other women are.

And what does John say? That Mary Magdalene went to the tomb alone.

When we look at the four Gospels side-by-side, we

see that there are some questions about the number of women who went to the tomb. Did Mary Magdalene go alone, as John suggests? Did a large group go, as Luke proposes? Or were there just a few, as Matthew and Mark indicate? We will attempt to answer these questions in a moment.

(2) WHEN DID THE WOMEN ARRIVE AT THE TOMB?

The four Gospels agree that the women arrived on the first day of the week, but as to the hour of their arrival, there are some contradictions.

Matthew tells us the women arrived slightly before daybreak: "After the sabbath, toward the dawn of the first day of the week...." (Matthew 28:1).

Mark, however, tells us they arrived *after* sunrise: "And very early on the first day of the week they went to the tomb when the sun had risen" (Mark 16:2).

Luke seems to agree with Matthew: the women arrived "on the first day of the week, at early dawn...." (Luke 24:1).

But John seems to suggest something very different: he clearly states that Mary Magdalene "came to the tomb early, while it was still dark" (John 20:1).

The contradictions about when the women arrived at the tomb are easily explained. Each of them, wrapped up within their own sorrow, would have remember the time of their arrival in a slightly different manner, and the way they told their stories would depend largely upon the dominant images within their own minds. But what each account agrees upon is that they arrived early in the morning, around daybreak. Do we really need a more precise time to believe the different accounts?

(3) WHAT DID THE WOMEN SEE, HEAR, AND DO?

Once again, we see the Gospels agreeing and disagreeing about the same event. They agree that the women were greeted by at least one angel, but they disagree as to what exactly happened.

In the Gospel of Matthew, an earthquake announced the descent of an angel who rolled back the stone and sat upon it. This event caused the guards to fall over as if they were dead. The angel turns to the women and says, "Do not be afraid; for I know that you seek Jesus who was crucified. He is not here; for he has risen, as he said. Come, see the place where he lay. Then go quickly and tell his disciples that he has risen from the dead, and behold, he is going before you to Galilee; there you will see him. Lo, I have told you" (Matthew 28:5–7). The women depart after this event ... only to encounter the risen Lord!

In Mark's Gospel, there is no mention of an earthquake, no mention of the guard, and the women arrive to find the stone already rolled away. They enter the tomb and see an angel sitting on the right. The angel gives them the same command we find in the Gospel of

Matthew. But instead of meeting the risen Jesus, the women leave, afraid.

Luke tells us that the stone had been rolled away when the women arrive at the tomb, so they go inside. The tomb is empty. Then two angels appear, and they seem to chastise the women: "Why do you seek the living among the dead? He is not here, but has risen. Remember how he told you, while he was still in Galilee, that the Son of man must be delivered into the hands of sinful men, and be crucified, and on the third day rise" (Luke 24:5–7). The women leave the tomb and seek out Jesus's disciples. There is no mention of them encountering the risen Jesus.

The Gospel of John provides us with completely different information. Mary Magdalene arrives at the tomb alone while it is dark. She sees that the stone has been rolled away. She runs to tell Peter and John that someone has stolen Jesus's body. Peter and John race to the tomb, leaving Mary behind. But she returns to the tomb. She stands outside weeping for a minute, then bends over to look inside. Two angles appear in the tomb, "sitting where the body of Jesus had lain," and they say to her, "Woman, why are you weeping?" (John 20:12–13). She must have been startled, for instead of addressing the angels, she turns around and encounters the risen Jesus, whom she recognizes—but only after he speaks her name. After this, she finds the disciples and tells them what happened.

(4) WHAT DID THE DISCIPLES DO?

It is significant that the disciples did not visit Jesus's tomb the first chance they had. Whether fear, humiliation, or despair kept them away, we can be sure their love of Jesus was not as intense as the women's love, for, as St Paul tells us, love conquers all things—even the most devastating of emotions.

And so, despite their discrepancies, the Gospels all agree that the women were given the task of seeking out the disciples to tell them the Lord had risen. How did the disciples respond to the women's testimony?

Matthew provides no information. After telling us that the women met the risen Jesus, he shifts viewpoints, and we learn of the exchange between the guards and the Jewish authorities. After this, we see the disciples with Jesus on a mountain in Galilee. Now Galilee is a four-day journey from Jerusalem, so this encounter did not happen on Easter Sunday.

The Gospel of Mark has difficulties that go beyond the scope of this book. The final part of the Gospel (Mark 16:9–20) is not the original ending. That ending was lost. The ending we now have was added later, perhaps in the second century, and its author used traditions found in the other Gospels: Jesus appears first to Mary Magdalene (from John); then he appears to two disciples traveling in the country (from Luke); finally, he appears to the apostles while they are eating supper (from both Luke and John).

The Gospel of Luke is the first to offer us concrete information. It seems the disciples did not believe the women. But Peter must have had his suspicions, for he ran to the tomb and found it empty. Luke also tells us about two disciples (neither one a member of the twelve) who, while traveling to Emmaus, encounter the risen Jesus. They do not recognize him at first, but once they do, they run back to Jerusalem to tell the twelve. When they arrive, they discover that Jesus has appeared to Peter. Moments later, he appears to the larger group.

We have already glimpsed at the Gospel of John. Mary Magdalene, upon finding the tomb empty, runs away and finds Peter and John. She tells them someone has stolen Jesus's body. They race to the tomb. John outruns Peter but does not enter until after Peter arrives and enters the tomb first. They find the tomb empty. Both leave. Later that day, Mary Magdalene finds the apostles again and tells them she's seen the risen Jesus. Later that evening, the risen Jesus appears to the apostles, who are hiding behind locked doors out of fear of the Jews.

SUMMARY

As we can see, the Gospels agree to the basic events. Women arrive at the tomb. They are met by angels who tell them Jesus has risen. They run off to tell the disciples. Peter runs to the tomb and finds it empty. Later in the day, the risen Jesus appears to the twelve. On these

essential points, Matthew, Mark, Luke, and John agree—
so we should not be so quick to doubt their testimony.

**Yes, they do agree, and things are a bit clearer now.
But there *are* differences, and I don't see how we can
reconcile them. Have you thought about this?**

I haven't thought too much about this, but Father Prat
did, and he attempted to "harmonize" the four Gospels,
much like how a police officer would reconstruct an accident based on different eyewitness testimony. Father
Prat's reconstruction is only one possible reconstruction,
though it is a good one. Of course, he assumes that
Matthew chose to combine separate events into one: the
angel rolling back the stone, the falling of the guards,
and the arrival of the women. (He did this for his own
narrative reasons, which, of course, fall outside the
scope of our conversation.) Given this one caveat, here's
how the events of the first Easter *may* have transpired:

1) Early in the morning, well before sunrise, an
earthquake announces the appearance of an angel. The
men guarding the tomb are overwhelmed with awe and
fall to the ground as if they were dead. When they come
to, they find the stone has been rolled away and the
tomb is empty. They flee out of fear.

2) A bit later, a group of women approach the tomb.
This group includes Mary Magdalene, Mary the mother

of James, Salome the wife of Zebedee and the mother of James and John, a woman named Joanna, and several other women.

3) They arrive to find that the stone has been moved and the tomb is empty. At this point, Mary Magdalene leaves the group and runs to tell the apostles that someone has stolen Jesus's body. She meets Peter and John, who upon hearing this news rush off to the tomb, leaving Mary behind.

4) Meanwhile, an angel appears to the women who remained at the tomb. The angel tells the women that Jesus has risen and that they are to tell his disciples. They leave, off to carry out their angelic mission.

5) Peter and John arrive at the tomb. They are alone. They assess the situation, then depart. Peter has his suspicions, but John believes the Lord is risen.

6) Mary Magdalene, distraught, decides to return to the tomb. She is alone. While she is there, two angels appear to her and ask her why she is weeping. A moment later, she encounters the risen Jesus. She believes him to be the gardener at first, but finally recognizes him. She falls and worships.

7) Meanwhile, two disciples set off to Emmaus. They have heard the women's story—that the tomb is empty, that angels appeared to them, that the angels said he has risen—but they have their doubts. While traveling, the risen Jesus begins to walk with them. Only after they arrive in Emmaus do they recognize him, and as soon as

they do so, he vanishes. They rush back to Jerusalem to tell the disciples.

8) Meanwhile, the risen Jesus appears to Peter, apparently alone. That is all we know of this encounter.

9) The disciples who had set off from Emmaus find the apostles. By now, it is evening. While telling the apostles what happened to them, Jesus appears in their midst.

And now we are at the end of the first Easter Sunday. This harmonization of the Gospels allows us to explain the differences between the narratives; it also allows us to see how the events might have unfolded. But it's important to remember that it may be wrong. The real point of this exercise was not to uncover what *really* happened, but to show that differences between the Gospels do not mean they are unreliable. One can make a solid argument as to how the differences can be reconciled.

In the end, this is all speculation. *Fun* speculation, but still speculation. Let us not forget that the Holy Spirit gave us four Gospels because we *need* four presentations of Jesus Christ. Each of these presentations exist in order to teach us what only one or two Gospels could not. Let's not get so caught up in harmonizing the Gospels that we forget to read them as individual books, each of which can teach us something beautiful about that first Easter morning.

We've established that Jesus of Nazareth existed, that the Gospels can be trusted, and that the Gospels proclaim that he has risen from the dead. But to believe a crucified man rose from the dead takes an incredible amount of trust. How can we possibly put so much trust in the what the apostles tell us?

That's an excellent question. We *are* dealing with an incredible claim, and the more we can provide reasons for believing this claim, the stronger our faith will be.

To help answer this question, I'd like to turn to a book entitled *Jesus Christ: The Fundamentals of Christology.* It was written by a former professor of mine, Father Roch Kereszty. Father Roch (as I know him) presents seven historical facts that "prove" Jesus rose from the dead (*Jesus Christ,* pp. 34–36). We're going to look at six of them—all of which deal with what the apostles did or what they experienced. They are:

1. The apostles' reaction to the death of Jesus.
2. Their proclamation of the risen Jesus.
3. The "proof" of the empty tomb.
4. The "proof" of other eyewitnesses.
5. Their personal transformation.
6. Their martyrdoms.

These six historical facts, taken collectively, offer

rock-solid evidence that we can trust what the apostles say about the resurrection of Jesus.

(1) THE DEATH OF CHRIST

First, let's consider how the apostles would have been affected by Jesus's death. To begin with, it's important to remember that Jesus did not simply die. He was arrested, tried, beaten, mocked, and executed—by being nailed to two pieces of wood.

The manner of his death would have greatly scandalized the apostles. They believed he was the Messiah. Peter, the leader of the twelve, professed that Jesus was "the Son of the living God" (Matthew 16:16). They thought he was the one sent by God to save the Jews from Roman affliction and to bring about a new and definitive glory to Israel. His public execution by the very people he was supposed to conquer would have shattered their faith in him. Jesus's crucifixion would not only have disabused them of their ideas about him, but it would have severed any possible desire to maintain these ideas. The crucifixion would have caused them to undergo a profound reversal of thought: it would have forced them to stop thinking one way about their Master and compelled them to start thinking another way.

We see hints that this reversal of thought had already happened in the hearts of the two disciples on the road to Emmaus. Let us set the stage. It is the Sunday after

Jesus was killed. A stranger approaches and asks what they are talking about. (This stranger is the risen Jesus.) The disciples say they are talking about the death of Jesus of Nazareth, and one says, "We had hoped that he was the one to redeem Israel" (Luke 24:21). Note the past tense: they *had* hoped. But now that Jesus is dead, that hope no longer remains.

Also, let us speculate on the profound humiliation his apostles must have suffered as they came to grips with their grief. These are men who had left everything to follow Jesus: their homes, their friends, their wives and children, their livelihoods. At some point, these are men who might have flaunted their status as being part of the Messiah's inner circle; after all, they did argue about who would be the greatest in Jesus's kingdom. But the Romans had proven that their sacrifices had been in vain. The Romans showed them to be utter fools. Imagine how they must have felt when they thought about returning to their homes, rebuilding their lives, and facing the people they left behind. The humiliation had to have been ever so deep.

Finally, we know they were afraid. After Judas betrayed Jesus, nine of the apostles fled out of fear. Only Peter and John stayed close to Jesus: they returned to Jerusalem, entered the high priest's courtyard, and witnessed some of Jesus's trial (John 18:15–16). But Peter denied Jesus three times because he feared to be associated with a condemned man (Matthew 26:69–75). Only John stayed close to Jesus until the end (John

19:17–37). But after the end had come, all of the apostles remained in hiding "for fear of the Jews" (John 20:19).

Fear, humiliation, shattered hopes—these were the emotions that gripped the hearts of the apostles on the morning of the first Easter Sunday. Not exactly emotions conducive to believing that Jesus had risen.

(2) THE PROCLAMATION OF THE APOSTLES

Fifty days after the tomb was found empty, the apostles started to preach that Jesus of Nazareth had risen from the dead. Father Roch makes an important point about their preaching:

> They do not merely affirm that his teaching, his personal influence, or "his cause" continues in the way that a great artist or a founder of religion may live on in his disciples. Rather they announce his bodily Resurrection and believe that Jesus, in a transformed spiritual body, personally lives in God, and among and with his disciples. (*Jesus Christ*, p. 34)

Just as Jesus pointed to himself, we see the central Christian message pointing toward Jesus. The apostles did not say, "Even though he is dead, it would be good to remember what he taught." Rather, they said, "He is no longer dead, but he has risen!" The resurrection of

Jesus becomes *the central component* of their preaching (for example, see Acts 2:29–32; 10:39–41).

(3) THE EMPTY TOMB

The empty tomb is a historical fact that has never been denied. For the sake of clarity, let's look at the sequence of events surrounding the tomb. To do so, we shall follow the Gospel of Matthew.

1) After Jesus died, Joseph of Arimathea—a rich man, and a member of the Jewish ruling class—obtained permission from Pilate to take Jesus's body into custody. Joseph then placed Jesus's body in his own new tomb (Matthew 27:57–61).

2) The Jewish leaders petitioned Pilate to have Roman soldiers guard Jesus's tomb. Their rationale? They knew Jesus had said he would rise in three days. They wanted the tomb guarded so that Jesus's disciples could not steal his body and then proclaim him to be risen from the dead (Matthew 27:62–63).

3) Pilate refused to place Roman soldiers at the tomb. He told the Jewish leaders to use their own soldiers to guard the tomb. This they did (Matthew 27:65–66).

4) The Jewish soldiers witnessed a celestial event that caused them to become "like dead men" (Matthew 28:2–4).

5) Upon waking, the soldiers went to the Jewish leaders and told them what had happened. The Jewish

leaders paid off the soldiers and told them to say, "His disciples came by night and stole him away while we were asleep." And they did as they were told (Matthew 28:1–15).

6) The story that the apostle stole Jesus's body in order to proclaim that he rose from the dead was still circulating among the Jews when Matthew wrote his gospel (Matthew 28:15)—which might have been as early as six or seven years after Jesus's death and resurrection.

This sixth point is most important, for it tells us that no one has ever denied that Jesus's tomb was empty. How could they? An empty tomb is, well, empty. There is either a body in it or there isn't. And given the fact that the tomb belonged to a rich member of the Jewish ruling class, the disciples couldn't have pointed to a different tomb. So, instead of denying it, the Jews put a different spin on it; they offered what today we call "fake news." Yes, the tomb is empty, but his disciples *stole his body!*

Now, the empty tomb is important for one essential reason. The empty tomb is in Jerusalem, the same city where Jesus died—*and* the same city were the apostles began preaching that he had risen from the dead. As Father Roch notes, their preaching

> could not have been maintained ... for a single day, for a single hour, if the emptiness of the tomb had not been established as a fact for all concerned. If the

opponents of the nascent Church could have pointed to the corpse of Jesus in the tomb, it would have completely discredited the message of the Resurrection in Jerusalem. (*Jesus Christ*, p. 35)

You simply can't say a man has risen from the dead when you have his corpse in front of you.

(4) EYEWITNESS TESTIMONY

Those who originally preached that Jesus had risen from the dead claimed to have seen the risen Christ. In fact, if there is one thing the Gospels agree on, it's that the risen Christ appeared to his apostles.

But he also appeared to Mary Magdalene (John 20), to the two disciples on the road to Emmaus (Luke 24), to Paul as he stormed toward Damascus to persecute the early Church (Acts 9), and "to more than five-hundred brethren at one time" (1 Corinthians 15:6). Think about that last bit of information for a moment—*hundreds* claimed to have seen the risen Jesus. And all of them could have corroborated the apostles' testimony!

It's Paul who tells us that the risen Jesus appeared to more than five-hundred at one time. And then he adds this intriguing phrase: "most of whom are still alive." Why is this phrase intriguing? Because eyewitness testimony was—and still is—the greatest proof that an event happened. Even though the New Testament is silent about who these witnesses were, we should not think they were unimportant in the apostolic Church. They may not have been leaders, but they would have been known, and they would have been sought out. The more eyewitness testimony available, the easier it is for those who were not witnesses to believe.

(5) THE TRANSFORMATION OF THE APOSTLES

We must not forget how the apostles reacted to the death of Christ: they went into hiding out of fear. But less than two months later, in the same city in which their Master was executed, they started to proclaim—without fear—that Jesus of Nazareth had risen from the dead. And this is only the beginning.

Read Acts of the Apostles and you will see that *nothing* could deter the twelve. They stood before the same Jewish leaders who crucified Christ and defended their mission to preach that Jesus had risen. They were imprisoned and scourged for preaching the risen Jesus. Not even the public stoning of one of their converts (Stephen) persuaded them to stop preaching the risen Jesus. Instead, they expanded their mission: they preached the risen Jesus in Samaria, in Gentile territory, and all throughout the Roman Empire.

Let's now consider Saint Paul. He himself underwent a profound change, from leader of the first Christian persecution to the greatest missionary of the apostolic Church. What caused this change? He had an experience of the risen Jesus (Acts 9). Afterward, he traveled throughout the Mediterranean world preaching the gospel, for which he suffered the following:

> Five times I have received at the hands of the Jews the forty lashes less one. Three times I have been beaten with rods; once I was stoned. Three times I have been shipwrecked; a night and a day I have been adrift at sea; on frequent journeys, in danger from rivers, danger from robbers, danger from my own people, danger from Gentiles, danger in the city, danger in the wilderness, danger at sea, danger from false brethren; in toil and hardship, through many a sleepless night, in hunger and thirst, often without food, in cold and exposure. (2 Corinthians 11:24–27)

This is a man who endured suffering. Why? Because he preached the risen Jesus.

Now here's the question: who would endure this kind of pain for a lie or a delusion? Their lives are the greatest proof of the truth of their message.

(6) THE APOSTLES SUFFERED MARTYRDOM

Almost every apostle suffered death for preaching the risen Jesus. And where they suffered death is an indication of how far they traveled to proclaim the risen Jesus.

In Rome, after years of enduring house arrest, Paul is beheaded between 64–67, during the reign of Nero.

In the same city, and around the same time, Peter

was crucified upside-down, at his own request. Why? Because he did not consider himself worthy to die in the same way as the Lord.

In Greece, Andrew was tied to an X-shaped cross on which he suffered two days before dying.

In Jerusalem, King Herod—the same man who beheaded John the Baptist and played a minor role in Jesus's crucifixion—had James the Greater murdered with the sword (Acts 12:2).

In the Egyptian city of Heliopolis, around AD 54, Philip was crucified.

In India, Bartholomew suffered tremendously—tradition says he suffered crucifixion, another says he was skinned alive—before he was finally beheaded.

Also in India, Thomas was run through with spears by the natives.

In Ethiopia, Matthew was stabbed in the back because he was critical of the king's morality.

James the Less was killed at the age of ninety-four with a club to his head.

In either Turkey or Greece, Jude was crucified at the age of seventy-two.

And Simon the Zealot made it all the way to modern-day England preaching the risen Christ, and it was there he was crucified.

Of the original twelve, only two didn't suffer martyrdom. Judas Iscariot took his own life. And John died naturally at a very old age in the city of Ephesus.

This means that ten of the original twelve died for

preaching the risen Jesus, and that Paul, the leader of the first Christian persecution, also died for preaching the risen Jesus (Kiger, "How Did the Apostles Die?").

What does all of this mean?

As Father Roch argues, the apostles' "martyrdom guarantees their good faith. [...]. But who would voluntarily accept dying for what he knows to be a hoax?" (*Jesus Christ*, 36).

To this rock-solid piece of logic we can add an observation made by Pope John Paul II: accepting the word of the martyrs saves us from long and exhausting intellectual endeavor (such as reading a book!). As John Paul II says,

Any number of examples could be found to demonstrate [the truth of a person]; but I think immediately of the martyrs, who are the most authentic witnesses to the truth about existence. The martyrs know that they have found the truth about life in the encounter with Jesus Christ, and nothing and no-one could ever take this certainty from them. Neither suffering nor violent death could ever lead them to abandon the truth which they have discovered in the encounter with Christ. This is why to this day the witness of the martyrs continues to arouse such interest, to draw agreement, to win such a hearing and to invite emulation. *This is why their word inspires such confidence: from the moment they speak to us of what we perceive deep down as the truth we have sought for so long, the martyrs provide evidence of a love that has no need of lengthy arguments in order to convince.* The martyrs stir in us a profound trust because they give voice to what we already feel and they declare what we would like to have the strength to express. (*Faith and Reason,* no. 32; emphasis added.)

Simply stated, the violent death the apostles suffered because they taught that Jesus had risen gives a profound weight to the authenticity and reliability of their word.

We can trust what they say because they died for it.

So there it is, rock-solid proof that Jesus rose from the dead!

Well, I'm not so sure we should phrase it like that. We certainly have rock-solid reasons to believe that Jesus has risen from the dead. We have established what Father John Hardon would call a "credible faith." But proof? I suppose from one point of view, Jesus's resurrection can be proved like any other historical event can be proved: from eyewitness testimony. But from another point of view, the resurrection of Jesus lies beyond the possibility of proof, for his resurrection lies beyond history itself. I think it's important to reflect a moment on this profound reality.

So far, we've only looked at the historical evidence surrounding the resurrection of Jesus. We've not looked at what the New Testament actually says about the resurrection. What does the New Testament say? That the resurrection of Jesus was fundamentally different from all other resurrections.

The Gospel tells us that Jesus raised people from the dead: the daughter of Jairus (Mark 5:21–43); the son of the mother of Nain (Luke 7:11–17); and Lazarus, the brother of Mary and Martha (John 11:1–44). In each of these cases, the person who was raised returned to his or her former life. It was as if they had merely fallen asleep for an extended period and Jesus had merely awakened them. In fact, that is how Jesus himself sees it. "Do not weep," he tells the family and friends of Jairus, "for she is not dead but sleeping" (Luke 8:52). But the New Testament speaks of Jesus's resurrection in a very different way.

First, his followers did not immediately recognize him. Mary Magdalene thought he was the gardener, and the disciples on the road to Emmaus thought he was a stranger.

Second, Jesus's resurrected body defies the laws of nature. He passes through locked doors. He seems to appear out of the blue. While his body is glorified, it still bears scars from his death. He vanishes at will.

Third, the way the risen Jesus relates to the apostles is different from how he related to them before his death. Beforehand, they traveled together and ate together. But afterward, the apostles are alone, without Jesus; when he appears, it is only for a time, and then he departs. Furthermore, he chooses who sees him and who does not (Acts 10:41).

Fourth, unlike the others he raised from the dead, the risen Jesus does not suffer a "second death" in order to complete his life on earth. Rather, he ascends into heaven. The apostles understood the risen Jesus to have conquered death and to have risen to a new kind of life —a life that does not end. As Saint Paul tells us,

> But in fact Christ as been raised from the dead, the first fruits of those who have fallen asleep. [...]. What is sown is perishable, what is raised is imperishable. It is sown in dishonor, it is raised in glory. It is sown in a physical body, it is raised in a spiritual body. (1 Corinthians 15:20, 42–44.)

Fifth, because Jesus has overcome death, has risen to a new life in God, and has ascended to the Father, the New Testament describes our relationship with the risen Jesus in a way that transcends time and space. "It is no longer I who live," Saint Paul tells us, "but Christ who lives in me" (Galatians 2:20). As Pope Benedict XVI writes,

> Essential, then, is the fact that Jesus's Resurrection was not just about some deceased individual coming back to life at a certain point, but that an ontological

leap occurred, one that touches being as such, opening up a new dimension that affects us all, creating for all of us a new space of life, a new space of being in union with God. (*Holy Week*, p. 274.)

What is the Pope telling us? The key to this passage is the phrase, "ontological leap." What does this phrase mean? The word "ontological" refers to being or existence, and so the phrase, "ontological leap" refers to a leap in being, a jump in existence.

Catholic theologians use this phrase to explain how the theory of evolution still requires God, for only God can bring about a "jump" in existence. They point out that there are three jumps in existence that science and evolution cannot explain:

1. That something comes from nothing.
2. That living things come from non-living things.
3. That rational intelligence comes from non-rational intelligence.

At each of these moments, an ontological leap occurred. In other words, the almighty God elevated existence, raised it to a higher level.

With this background in mind, let's return to what Pope Benedict said—that the resurrection of Jesus brought about an ontological leap. In other words, his resurrection brings about a *jump in human existence*. It raises humanity to a higher level, one in which we transcend the confines of space and time, of aging and death, and enter into a new kind of life, a resurrected and glorious life—a life made possible only in Christ, through Christ, and with Christ.

This is lofty and abstract language, so let's use figurative language that can help us see the truth of what we're saying. To help us, let's turn once again to the work of Saint Paul:

What is sown is perishable, what is raised is imperishable. It is sown in dishonor, it is raised in glory. It is sown in weakness, it is raised in power. It is sown a physical body, it is raised a spiritual body. If there is a physical body, there is also a spiritual body. Thus it is written, "The first man Adam became a living being"; the last Adam became a life-giving spirit. But it is not the spiritual which is first but the physical, and then the spiritual. The first man was from the earth, a man of dust; the second man is from heaven. As was the man of dust, so are those who are of the dust; and as is the man of heaven, so are those who are of heaven. Just as we have borne the image of the man of dust, we shall also bear the image of the man of heaven. I tell you this, brethren: flesh and blood cannot inherit the kingdom of God, nor does the perishable inherit the imperishable.

Lo! I tell you a mystery. We shall not all sleep, but we shall all be changed, in a moment, in the twinkling of an eye, at the last trumpet. For the trumpet will sound, and the dead will be raised imperishable, and we shall be changed. For this perishable nature must put on the imperishable, and this mortal nature must put on immortality. When the perishable puts on the imperishable, and the mortal puts on immortality, then shall come to pass the saying that is written: "Death is swallowed up in victory. O death, where is thy victory? O death, where is thy sting?" The sting of death is sin, and the power of sin is the law. But thanks be to God, who gives us the victory through our Lord Jesus Christ. Therefore, my beloved brethren, be steadfast, immovable, always abounding in the work of the Lord, knowing that in the Lord your labor is not in vain. (1 Corinthians 15:42–58)

What is Saint Paul telling us? That our lives on this plane of existence (earth) are destined for a higher plane of existence (heaven). Here, we are mortal, and we must leave this life in a "dishonorable" way, that is, by death. But through Jesus, we shall conquer death: we shall be raised to glory, and we shall be immortal. We shall undergo a jump in existence, an ontological leap, a complete transformation! In a phrase, we shall be raised to a new life with God.

This is why we cannot limit the resurrection of Jesus to a mere historical fact, for his resurrection takes us outside the limits of history and gives us a hope that transcends history itself. Therefore, the resurrection of

Jesus is a matter of *both* reason *and* faith. It's a matter of reason because we can provide rational grounds for believing it happened, but it's a matter of faith because we must believe what the New Testament says about the *meaning* of the resurrection: to believe that Jesus is risen is to believe that he is the first fruits of a *new* creation.

As Father Roch points out, to believe in the resurrected Jesus is to believe that "he has been transformed by God's Spirit into a new man ... the final creation." It is to believe that in Jesus "our history has reached its end and goal," that "he is the firstborn of many brothers," and that his resurrection is a sign of our "radical new beginning" in God (*Jesus Christ,* p. 46). To proclaim that Jesus Christ is risen from the dead is to proclaim that God has changed everything.

4

WHY WE BELIEVE IN THE CATHOLIC CHURCH

I feel a little lost in the forest. Before moving to our last question, could we get a bird's-eye view of our overall plan?

Our overall plan can be summed up in the questions we discussed in Chapter Two:

1. Does God exist?
2. Has God revealed himself?
3. Is his revelation found in the Catholic Church?

We've answered the first question: yes, God exists. We've answered the second question: yes, we know God has revealed himself because Jesus of Nazareth is risen from the dead. All of that being said, we still have one final point to consider—at least in terms of building solid foundations for our faith. That's the third question: Is God's revelation found in the Catholic Church?

Or, stated in another way (which gives a different emphasis), we can ask, "How do we know that the Catholic Church is the one, true Church established by Jesus Christ?"

I'm reminded of a question I've been asked before: "What difference does it make what church someone is going to so long as he is going to church?" Isn't that a valid point of view?

No, it's not. Let's consider what Jesus Christ did for us. He taught us the truth necessary for salvation, and he suffered and died so that we might be saved. These two realities—his words and his actions—complement one another: his words explain his actions, and his actions prove his words. But they also complement one another on a deeply theological level, and one that has incredible meaning for us: through his death and resurrection he offers us the gift of salvation, and through his words he teaches us what we must do in order to accept this gift. How do we accept the gift he obtained through his death? By understanding his teachings and living them out in our own daily lives. But how is that possible if there are contradictory interpretations of what he said and did?

For example, Jesus said that "unless one is born again, he cannot see the kingdom of heaven" (John 3:3; *New King James Version*). You can't find a serious Christian —Catholic, Orthodox, or Protestant—who doesn't understand and agree with the most basic meaning of this statement, namely, that we need to be transformed in order to be saved. But *how* does this transformation come about—through the sacrament of Baptism, or by accepting Jesus as your personal Lord and Savior? Another example: Jesus told Peter that he, Peter, would be the rock upon which he, Jesus, would build his church (Matthew 16:18). Again, all Christians accept the primacy Peter had among the disciples, but does this primacy get passed down to a successor whom we call the pope?

These are just two critical differences that divide the Body of Christ, and they can be multiplied to include the role of the saints, the relationship between Sacred Tradition and Sacred Scripture, the development of doctrine, the sacraments and sacramentals, devotion to Blessed Virgin Mary, the existence of purgatory and whether we can "pray for the dead," and finally, the theology of the Eucharist and the holy sacrifice of the Mass. And these are just the Catholic doctrines that Protestants do not accept. Protestantism has its own set of doctrines that Catholics do not accept. Furthermore, the reason there are roughly 200 official Protestant denominations in the

United States alone is that they can't agree about what Jesus said and did.

Let's add to this utter mess one rather alarming fact —Jesus himself prayed that we would *not* be divided. On the night before he died, he offered a prayer for unity: "Father, keep them in thy name ... that they may be one, even as we are one" (John 17:11). Just as the Father and the Son are united, so too, Christians are to be united. How are the Father and Son united? To use technical theological terms, they are united in intellect and will. To use language that makes more sense to us, they are united in mind and heart. And so, Christians are to have a unity of mind: we are to see and understand Christ's teachings in the same way. And we are to have a unity of heart: we are to desire and love the same things. Practically, this means that we need to be unified in what we believe about God (doctrine) and how we worship God (the liturgy).

So: the idea that it doesn't matter which church people attend so long as they attend some church belies the truth that Christ's teaching is essential for salvation, it ignores the incredible differences between the Christian denominations, and it contradicts the will of Christ himself. The community established by Jesus and the apostles was a community of one mind and one heart, a Church unified in intellect and will. This Church is the one founded by Christ. All other churches and Christian communities have broken away from this one, true Church.

So, why do we believe in the Catholic Church? How do we know she is the one, true Church established by Jesus Christ?

Remember how we noted that God puts signs of his existence in creation? And remember how we took that idea and applied it to his revelation—namely, that if God had revealed himself, he would give us a sign of his revelation? We can do something similar here: we can look for a sign that points to the truth of the Catholic Church.

This sign would need to be a teaching that fundamentally separates Catholicism from the other branches of Christianity; it would need to be a stumbling block, a source of division. And it would need to be evident in the teaching of Christ and throughout Church history.

Of all the teachings of the Catholic Church, only one fits this description. It has nothing to do with the Eucharist, the saints, or the Blessed Mother, for Orthodox Christians believe in all three. It has everything to do with the pope, for the pope is the reason Eastern Orthodoxy split from Rome, and the pope is one of the reasons why the Protestant Reformation happened.

What makes the Catholic Church distinct from Orthodoxy and Protestantism is what she believes about the pope—namely, that he is the Vicar of Christ here on earth (*Catechism*, no. 882). If we can demonstrate that the primacy of the pope is both a biblical and historical doctrine, as well as a logical doctrine to believe to be true, we can establish credible grounds for believing that the Catholic Church is the Church established by Jesus Christ. We can build a firm foundation for our faith in the Church.

What's a "vicar," and what does the Church mean by "Vicar of Christ"?

The English word "vicar" comes from the Latin word, *vicarius*. In Latin, *vicarius* has both a noun and a verb form, and both forms have the same meaning. As a noun it means "substitute," and as a verb it means "acting on behalf of another."

Therefore, when the Church says that the pope is the Vicar of Christ, she means that he is the substitute for Christ and that he has the ability to act on behalf of Christ, in the name of Christ, and with the authority of Christ (*Catechism*, no. 561). The Church believes this because she believes that the pope is the successor of Saint Peter, and that Jesus made Peter his representative.

If I were to tell my Protestant family members that

I'm Catholic because the pope is the representative of Christ on earth, they would respond, "Where do you find that in the Bible?" Do you have an answer for that?

We need to answer that question in two steps. First, we need to show that Jesus made Peter his representative, and second, we need to show that the pope is the successor of Peter.

But we immediately run into a problem your Protestant family members would say disproves Catholicism. It's this: nowhere in the Bible does it say that the pope is the successor of Peter; at least, the Bible never directly says this. Nowhere in the New Testament do we read that Linus (the second pope) received the authority of Peter, that this authority was passed down to Anacletus, then to Clement, then to Evaristus, and through the ages to Francis. So, in a way, we are handcuffed by the request to prove *from the Bible* that the pope is the Vicar of Christ. We can show that Jesus made Peter his representative, but we can't directly show that this "Petrine authority" (as we Catholics think of it) was passed down to any successor.

On the other hand, we can—and should—challenge the Protestant insistence to "prove" every doctrine from the Bible. This insistence is rooted in their doctrine of *sola Scriptura*, which says that the Bible is the sole authority for Christian faith and practice. But this doctrine is hardly tenable. While it's off topic, it is worth our time discussing why *sola Scriptura* should not only be questioned but outright rejected. As I see it, there are four basic problems with *sola Scriptura*.

(1) THE PROBLEM OF THE CANON

In this context, the word "canon" refers to an authoritative list of books, and here we are, of course, talking about the books of the Bible. If *sola Scriptura* was correct—if it is the sole authority of Christian faith—then somewhere in the Bible we should find a list of books that belong to it. After all, the canon of Scripture is part of Christian faith. But, alas, no such list exists.

This raises a particularly thorny problem for any Protestant: how do we know, say, that Romans belongs in the Bible? How do we know the Gospel of John belongs? Who decided on these books and all of the others? Who gave this person the authority to make such sweeping decisions? Do we find his name in the Bible? Do we see Jesus giving this person this kind of authority?

Let's remember that Martin Luther—the man who stood at the vanguard of the Reformation—started Protestantism by *removing* books from the Old Testament, books that Christians had read for over a thousand years. What's to stop a new Martin Luther from removing more books? Or perhaps even adding some?

Why can we not add the Gospel of Thomas or the Apocalypse of Paul to the New Testament?

Unless there is an authoritative list that tells us which books belong in the Bible, the canon of Scripture is threatened by the winds of change whenever they decide to gust. Protestants maintain that the lists of Old Testament and New Testament books are set, but who had the authority to create the lists in the first place?

What all of this means is that Protestants rely upon an authoritative tradition *greater than* the Bible to tell them which books belong in the Bible. Of course, this tradition itself can be questioned: what makes it authoritative? And we might also ask Protestants another question: why do you accept this one tradition but not others? In other words, the whole idea of *sola Scriptura* is rendered nonsensical once you begin analyzing where the canon of Scripture came from and why its source is authoritative.

(2) THE PROBLEM OF TIME

For the sake of simple math, let's assume Christ died in AD 30. Saint Paul did not start writing until 50, and John did not write his Gospel until 90. This means that the New Testament did not exist until *at least* sixty years after the death and resurrection of Jesus.

I emphasize the phrase, "at least," because it would take time for books of the New Testament to be hand copied, disseminated to the early Christian churches, and collected into a unified whole. How much time? We can only guess, but even if it was only a few years, the problem of time still undermines the Protestant claim. For if Christian faith and practice is based on the authority of the Bible alone, how, exactly, does Christianity exist without a New Testament?

(3) THE PROBLEM OF ILLITERACY

There were two reasons why *sola Scriptura* spread like wildfire in the sixteenth century: first, the printing press allowed books to be copied easily and cheaply, and second, with the proliferation of books came the spread of literacy. This is only logical, for what would be the point of reading if there were no books to read? Cheap books meant a lot of books, and a lot of books meant an increased desire to read. But what of the centuries before the printing press? What of the first, second, and third centuries of the Christian era, when Christianity was still spreading?

By all estimates, the literacy rate was between five and ten percent. Concretely, this meant that in a Christian community of a hundred, only about five or ten members could read. Or to state this in another way, it meant that over ninety members were *unable* to access the sole authority of their faith—the Bible. What does that mean? It means that they had to rely upon others to tell them what the Bible said, and it means they had no way of knowing if the members of the literate class were telling them the truth about what the Bible said.

In other words, for at least ninety percent of Christians, the Church leaders were the sole authority of Christian faith and practice. It could be no other way, for *sola Scriptura* is impossible for an illiterate culture.

(4) THE PROBLEM OF CONTRADICTION

The claim that the Bible alone is the sole source of authority is contradicted by the Bible itself. For example, Saint Paul tells Timothy that the church is "the pillar and foundation of the truth" (1 Timothy 3:15, *New International Version*). Unlike Jesus, who always pointed toward himself as the source of truth, Scripture points away from itself and says that the Church is the source of truth.

Another example: Paul tells the Thessalonians to "stand firm and hold fast to the teachings we passed on to you, whether by word of mouth or by letter" (2 Thessalonians 2: 15, *New International Version*). Why would he say such a thing?

Other than Romans, Paul wrote all of his letters to churches he had visited. These weren't quick, two-hour visits, either. Rather, it's likely he stayed with these communities for weeks; according to Acts of the Apostles, he stayed a "long time" in Iconium (14:3). So perhaps we should think in terms of months.

Why did Paul write churches he had already visited? Because he heard of problems within the communities. The believers in Thessalonica were concerned they had missed the return of Christ. The believers in Galatia struggled to find harmony between Jewish Christians and Gentile Christians. And the believers in Corinth ... well, they had more problems than we can list. It's because of these problems that Paul wrote, and he wrote in order to remind them of what he had taught them. But this does not mean that he filled his letters with everything he taught them. Galatians can be read in less than thirty minutes, and certainly Paul stayed in Galatia longer than that. Even his longest letter (Romans) is shorter than three of the Gospels, the Acts of the Apostles, and the Book of Revelation. A short letter simply cannot contain the breadth and depth of all that he taught the different churches he visited.

Rather, he was selective when he wrote, choosing those teachings that addressed the problems of that community. But there was also an entire body of oral teaching he had given them, and he reminded the Thessalonians of this oral teaching when he told them to "stand firm and hold fast to the teachings we passed on to you, whether by word of mouth or by letter."

Are we to assume that since he did not write down this oral teaching, the apostolic Church ignored it as incidental? Are we to think they dismissed what he only said and did not write down as non-authoritative? That seems highly unlikely. Rather, it's logical to assume that these communities held fast to all of his teachings, and that these teachings became part of the Sacred Tradition of the Church. But the doctrine of *sola Scriptura* forces us to dismiss the idea that a body of oral teaching exists and that it was passed down from generation to generation.

In sum, the problem of the canon, the problem of time, the problem of illiteracy, and the problem of contradiction make *sola Scriptura* an untenable doctrine for any Christian.

(For more information, see Henry Graham, *Where We Got The Bible.*)

This explains why we Catholics accept Sacred Tradition as a valid source of Christian faith and practice, and that's good to know. But let's get back to the topic. Where in the Gospels do we see that Jesus made Peter his representative?

We find it at the end of the Gospel of John. We're all very familiar with this passage, and while we don't typically think of it as having anything to do with Peter's leadership role, the Church does (see *Catechism*, no. 553). It reads,

> When they had finished breakfast, Jesus said to Simon Peter, "Simon, son of John, do you love me more than these?" He said to him, "Yes, Lord; you know that I

love you." He said to him, "Feed my lambs." A second time he said to him, "Simon, son of John, do you love me?" He said to him, "Yes, Lord; you know that I love you." He said to him, "Tend my sheep." He said to him the third time, "Simon, son of John, do you love me?" Peter was grieved because he said to him the third time, "Do you love me?" And he said to him, "Lord, you know everything; you know that I love you." Jesus said to him, "Feed my sheep...." (John 21:15–17)

Too often when we think about this narrative we focus on the question-and-answer portion of the story. Three times does Jesus ask, *Do you love me?* and three times does Peter respond, *Lord, you know I love you.* We see in Peter's three acts of love an echo of the three times he denied knowing Jesus. By proclaiming his love of the Lord, he makes amends for his denial of knowing him; he is doing penance for his sins. When we look at the story in this way, we are looking at it correctly, but not completely. We are overlooking something rather important—how Jesus responds to Peter's response.

After every proclamation of love, Jesus gives Peter a command: "Feed my lambs ... tend my sheep ... feed my sheep...." What is going on here? To understand his response, we must remember that Jesus called himself the Good Shepherd. It would be well worth your time to read carefully all that Jesus says on the matter (John 10:1–18), but here, let us pare down the passage to only a handful of verses:

Truly, truly, I say to you, he who does not enter the sheepfold by the door but climbs in by another way, that man is a thief and a robber; but he who enters by the door is the shepherd of the sheep. I am the good shepherd. The good shepherd lays down his life for the sheep. He who is a hireling and not a shepherd, whose own the sheep are not, sees the wolf coming and leaves the sheep and flees; and the wolf snatches them and scatters them. He flees because he is a hireling and cares nothing for the sheep. I am the good shepherd; I know my own and my own know me, as the Father knows me and I know the Father; and I lay down my life for the sheep. So there shall be one flock, one shepherd.

We now have two distinct ideas to consider: first, the triple command to "feed his sheep" that Jesus gives to Peter, and second, his teaching that he is the Good Shepherd. Put these two together, and we see Jesus giving Peter the same task he took upon himself: Peter is to continue Jesus's mission of being the Good Shepherd.

That this command is given *after* his death and resurrection gives a profound weight to this interpretation. Jesus is about to ascend into heaven; physically, he will no longer be with his sheep (but he will be sacramentally present). Someone needs to stand in his place. Someone needs to act as the Good Shepherd on his behalf. Someone needs to feed Jesus's sheep, to tend Jesus's sheep, and to sacrifice his life, if necessary, for the good of Jesus's sheep. Jesus needs someone to be his representative after he is gone. Jesus needs someone to be his "vicar" here on earth. That someone is Peter.

We know where in the Gospels that Peter was appointed the "vicar" of Christ, but where does it say that this authority is passed down to his successors?

Let's turn to the Gospel of Matthew. Again, we are probably familiar with this passage, for it's when Jesus gives Peter the "keys of the kingdom." Now, it's not *directly* stated in the passage that Peter's authority is passed down to his successors, but it *is* there—if you know how to read the text.

To begin, let us place the passage firmly in our mind:

> Now when Jesus came into the district of Caesarea Philippi, he asked his disciples, "Who do men say that the Son of man is?" And they said, "Some say John the Baptist, others say Elijah, and others Jeremiah or one of the prophets." He said to them, "But who do you say that I am?" Simon Peter replied, "You are the Christ, the Son of the living God." And Jesus answered him, "Blessed are you, Simon Bar-Jona! For flesh and blood has not revealed this to you, but my Father who is in heaven. And I tell you, you are Peter, and on this

rock I will build my church, and the powers of death shall not prevail against it. I will give you the keys of the kingdom of heaven, and whatever you bind on earth shall be bound in heaven, and whatever you loose on earth shall be loosed in heaven." Then he strictly charged the disciples to tell no one that he was the Christ. (Matthew 16:13–20)

The story is simple enough to understand. Jesus asks the twelve two questions. Who do *people* say that I am? Who do *you* say that I am? Certainly, the twelve had talked among themselves, sharing their thoughts about Jesus with one another. These men had to have been deeply religious, for why else would they have left their lives to follow Jesus? And Jesus would have certainly known about their whisperings, as well as their most private thoughts, for he did have the ability to read hearts (*Catechism*, no. 473). So when he asked them, "Who do you say that I am?" he was not asking to obtain information. Rather, he knew it was time to establish the foundation on which he would build his Church.

PETER'S PROCLAMATION

Why do I claim that when he asked "Who do you say that I am?" Jesus was establishing the foundation for his Church? Because when Peter says, "You are the Christ, the Son of the living God," Jesus does not congratulate

Peter for his wisdom. He doesn't tell Peter how intelligent he is for a fisherman. He doesn't hold Peter up as the model of deep contemplation. Rather, he says, "Blessed are you, Simon Bar-Jona! For flesh and blood has not revealed this to you, but my Father who is in heaven." What does Jesus mean?

Peter was able to make such a profession of faith only because he received a special revelation from the Father. Peter didn't discern Jesus's true identity by himself; rather, God the Father enlightened his mind. Furthermore, this revelation was given to Peter. Which another way of saying that it was *not* given to James, Andrew, John, or any of the others. Another point: by this time in Jesus's public ministry, Peter had already emerged as the leader of the twelve. And so, from a certain point of view, it would be proper to speak of the Father *confirming* Peter's leadership, for the Father gave this revelation to Peter, and to Peter alone.

"YOU ARE ROCK"

Then Jesus says, "You are Peter, and on this rock I will build my church." Much can be said about this one passage.

First, Peter's real name is Simon, and Jesus renames him Peter. This is more important that we might first think. In the Old Testament, God renames a few people: Abram became Abraham; Sarai became Sarah; Jacob became Israel. In each case, the new name indicates the new role the person would play. Abram becomes the father of many nations. Sarai becomes the mother of the son of promise. Jacob becomes the one who wrestles with God and the father of God's chosen people. So when the Son of God renames Simon, he is indicating that Simon now has a new role—he will be the foundation of the Church. This truth becomes much more apparent with our next point, which focuses on the wordplay taking place in the passage.

Second, the name "Peter" comes from the Greek word *petra/petros* (it has both a feminine and masculine form). It means "rock." In the original Greek, the passage would read, "You are *petros*, and on this *petra* I will build my church." Or, in English: "You are rock, and on this rock I will build my church." It's a play on words that connects the man Simon with his new role as being the foundation of the Church.

Third, this play on words is magnified even more by the event's location. They were in Caesarea Philippi, and in Caesarea Philippi there is a giant hill that looks like a large rock, and upon this hill pagans would assemble to worship their gods. Given this backdrop, Jesus seems to be saying, "You, Simon, are like that rock over there, for upon you my people will come to worship me." In this light, Peter is more than the foundation of the Church. He is the "place" where people will come to worship, which is a poetic way of saying that only those united to Peter will worship God in spirit and truth.

THE KEYS OF THE KINGDOM

We now come to what will be for us the most important element of this passage. Jesus says to Peter, "I will give you the keys of the kingdom of heaven, and whatever you bind on earth shall be bound in heaven, and whatever you loose on earth shall be loosed in heaven." Here, Jesus is not speaking spontaneously, saying whatever comes to him at the moment. Rather, his words are deliberate, for he wants to direct the apostles' minds (and ours as well) to an Old Testament passage.

This passage comes from Isaiah (22:15–25). It tells of a man named Eliakim. Eliakim served in the royal cabinet of King Hezekiah, who ruled the Jews from 715–687 BC. We are going to look at only three verses from this long passage, so it would do us well to consider the larger context. Beginning in 22:15, we read that a man named Shebna had a high position in King Hezekiah's court; he was something like Hezekiah's prime minister —that is, he has all the authority of the king. But because of his pride, Shebna is ousted from this office. Now vacant, the office is given to Eliakim. Here is what Isaiah writes:

> In that day I will call my servant Eliakim the son of Hilkiah, and I will clothe him with your robe, and will bind your girdle on him, and will commit your authority to his hand; and he shall be a father to the inhabitants of Jerusalem and to the house of Judah.

And I will place on his shoulder the key of the house of David; he shall open, and none shall shut; and he shall shut, and none shall open. (Isaiah 22:20–22)

What are we being told? That the office of prime minister is empty, that Eliakim will now fill it, and that one of the symbols of this position is a key of the kingdom, a key that gives him the power to open and close. Again, poetic language is being used, but it means what you would think it means: Eliakim has the authority to make binding decisions in the name of the king.

With this Old Testament background, we are in a better position to understand the meaning of Peter and the keys. He was appointed the "prime minister" of the kingdom of God. He was given the power to bind and loose. He was given the authority of Christ the King here on earth. And implied in all of this is one final truth: when his office is empty, another must fulfill it. Peter's authority to bind and loose is given to his successors. (For more information, see Hahn, *Why Do We Have a Pope?*)

It's for this reason that we Catholics call Peter the first pope. He is the one who was given the authority of Christ. And when his office becomes empty, another must fill it.

But didn't Jesus give the power to bind and loose to

**the other apostles as well? What makes Peter
different?**

You're right. Shortly after he gave Peter the keys of the
kingdom, Jesus gave all of the apostles the power to
"bind and loose" (Matthew 18:18). Jesus, however,
didn't single out Andrew or James, Thomas or Philip; he
singled out Peter. Jesus didn't rename any of them; he
renamed only Simon. The Father didn't reveal Jesus's
true identity to Jude or Nathaniel; it was revealed to
Peter alone. And to Peter alone did he give the keys of
the kingdom, and only to Peter did he promise that the
gates of hell would not prevail. So: even though all of
the apostles share in the authority of Christ, Peter was
given primacy over the group. He would be their leader,
the one with absolute authority, and the one Jesus
would rely upon to lead his Church.

In fact, just a few hours before his arrest, we see
Jesus rely on Peter to lead the others. During the Last
Supper, after instituting the Eucharist, Jesus predicts
that one of the twelve will betray him. One by one, each
apostle denies that *he* could betray Jesus. They soon
begin arguing about which one of them is the greatest.
Jesus corrects them; he reminds them that the greatest
is to serve the rest. It's at this point, Jesus turns to Peter
and says:

Simon, Simon, behold, Satan demanded to have you,

that he might sift you like wheat, but I have prayed for you that your faith may not fail; and when you have turned again, strengthen your brethren. (Luke 22:31–32)

Reading this passage as it is, we are inclined to think that Jesus told Peter that the evil one had something special in mind for him alone. "The devil is going to test you, Peter," Jesus seems to say, "but I have prayed for you, and after your test, don't forget about the others." In the larger context of the Gospels, this seems like a good interpretation. Peter is the leader of the apostles, the rock upon which Jesus will build his Church. If the devil wanted to try any of the twelve, it would certainly be him. In fact, besides Judas, who did betray him, Peter is the only one who out-right rejected Jesus: "I do not know the man!" he cried out three times.

Now, as rational as this interpretation is, it is incorrect. The problem lies in English grammar. The word "you" can be either singular or plural. I can look at my son and say, "I want you to clean the kitchen," or I can look at all four of my kids and say, "I want you to clean the kitchen." Both would be grammatically correct. But it's confusing, as we all know, and this is why, when speaking to a group, we would say, "I want all of you to clean the kitchen"—or, "y'all," if you're from the South.

This grammatical point is of the utmost importance because Jesus alternates between the singular and the plural form of "you." His entire meaning depends on knowing when he uses the singular form of "you" and when he is using the plural form. Let's reread this passage, this time reading from the *New American Bible*:

> Simon, Simon, behold Satan has demanded to sift all of you like wheat, but I have prayed that your own faith may not fail; and once you have turned back, you must strengthen your brothers.

Satan has demanded to put *all twelve* to the test. But Jesus does not pray for the twelve. *He prays only for Peter.* He relies on Peter to stand in his (Jesus's) own place, to take care of his sheep, to give strength to the others. In this way, Peter begins his ministry of being the rock on which the Church is built shortly after the death of Jesus. So, going back to your question, while Peter and the apostles share in the authority of Christ, Peter is the leader of the apostles.

We can bring all of this to the present. Because Jesus gave the authority to bind and loose to all of the apostles, all bishops are successors to the apostles, just as the pope is the successor of Peter (*Catechism*, nos. 862, 880). But the pope is "head of the college of bishops" (*Catechism*, no. 881), and bishops have authority only because they are united to the pope (*Catechism*, no. 883). Thus, the relationship Christ established between Peter and the apostles continues today in relationship between the pope and the bishops.

You keep talking about how the pope and the bishops continue what Jesus began in Peter and the apostles. It seems we have moved squarely into the realm of apostolic succession. Is there any biblical proof that the apostles handed their authority to successors?

Come to think of it, there is. It's found in the first chapter of the Acts of the Apostles. Let's set the stage.

Just before he ascended into heaven, Jesus gave the twelve their mission: they were to preach the gospel to all nations, beginning in Judea. But he also told them they first needed to wait for the Spirit to give them power from on high. So they waited in Jerusalem, in the upper room, where they had celebrated the Last Supper. Let us now turn to the Acts of the Apostles.

In those days Peter stood up among the brethren (the company of persons was in all about a hundred and twenty), and said, "Brethren, the scripture had to be fulfilled, which the Holy Spirit spoke beforehand by the mouth of David, concerning Judas who was guide to those who arrested Jesus. For he was numbered among us, and was allotted his share in this ministry. [...]. For it is written in the book of Psalms, 'Let his habitation become desolate, and let there be no one to live in it'; and 'His office let another take.'

"So one of the men who have accompanied us

during all the time that the Lord Jesus went in and out among us, beginning from the baptism of John until the day when he was taken up from us—one of these men must become with us a witness to his resurrection." And they put forward two, Joseph called Barsabbas, who was surnamed Justus, and Matthias. And they prayed and said, "Lord, who knowest the hearts of all men, show which one of these two thou hast chosen to take the place in this ministry and apostleship from which Judas turned aside, to go to his own place." And they cast lots for them, and the lot fell on Matthias; and he was enrolled with the eleven apostles. (Acts 1:15–26)

We are told of the election of Matthias to fill Judas's empty seat. What should we make of this event? That the apostles realized their ministry does not end with death. Rather, it continues in the work of those who come after them. But not just any who come after, for the one who would take the place of an apostle must be appointed by the community.

In a similar way, if Peter was to be the foundation of the community of believers—if he had been selected to be Jesus's representative here on earth—is it not also logical to assume that this double mission to be the rock of the Church and the Vicar of Christ would continue after Peter's death?

In fact, we see a correlation here between Jesus and Peter, and Peter and his successors. When did Peter's ministry begin? After the death of Christ, when he was to strengthen his brethren. But in a fuller sense, Peter's ministry began after Jesus's ascension, which is the definitive end to Jesus's bodily presence here on earth (but not his sacramental presence in the Eucharist). With Jesus no longer present, Peter takes on the full role of being Christ's representative. And so Peter, as the leader of the Church, carries on his *singular* ministry until he dies. But the Church still needs Christ's vicar to feed and tend the sheep. Therefore, Peter's *singular* ministry is given to another—the pope. The pope carries within himself the incredible responsibility of the Petrine ministry.

Someone has to lead the Church, and it makes sense to me that the leadership belongs to Peter and his successors, and the apostles and their successors. But I can already hear what my Protestant friends will say. "You're making a lot of assumptions, but offering no proof." Can you offer any proof that this interpretation is valid?

I'm not sure we're making any assumptions. Are we not drawing logical and rational conclusions based on what we find in the Bible? But for the sake of establishing a realized faith built upon solid foundations, let's offer some proof.

To do so, we will need to move beyond the biblical witness to the witness of the Church Fathers—those great theologians who wrote between 100 and 650. From their writings, we can see how the early Church was structured. Now, it would be impossible to look at every passage the Fathers wrote about the pope. We have to limit ourselves to a few key passages. For the sake of simplicity, I've chosen three—one from each of the first three centuries of the Christian era. They each show, in their own way, that the Church held fast to apostolic succession and Petrine authority.

SAINT CLEMENT OF ROME

Our first passage, which was written around AD 95, is from the very first Church Father, Saint Clement of Rome (d. 99). If anyone should know anything about apostolic succession, it would be Clement, for he was Peter's fourth successor, which makes him the fourth pope. In fact, tradition tells us that Clement knew both Peter and Paul, which, in my opinion, is an astonishing fact to consider. At any rate, in this passage, he explains why the apostles left successors. He writes,

> Through countryside and city [the apostles] preached, and they appointed their earliest converts, testing them by the Spirit, to be the bishops and deacons of future believers. Nor was this a novelty, for bishops and deacons had been written about a long time

earlier... Our apostles knew through our Lord Jesus Christ that there would be strife for the office of bishop. For this reason, therefore, having received perfect foreknowledge, they appointed those who have already been mentioned and afterward added the further provision that, if they should die, other approved men should succeed to their ministry. (*Letter to the Corinthians* 42:4–5, 44:1–3)

Clement gives two reasons why the apostles appointed their successors. First, the apostles wanted to avoid "strife for the office of bishop." What does he mean? Two things. One: it eliminates any competition for the office. Even today, when the Church is in need of a new bishop, the job is not posted; priests do not send their applications to Rome. Rather, recommendations are made, the pope decides, and the newly appointed bishop is typically shocked that the pope even knew who he was. Two: if the apostles had a say in who became their successors, then the humble and holy would hold the office of bishop instead of the proud and ambitious. Of course, it has not always worked out that way. The history of the Church is filled with power-hungry bishops who have left their flock malnourished. But for every bad bishop, there are dozens of good bishops—and a few holy bishops—who sacrifice themselves for Christ's sheep. Now even though no individual bishop appoints his own successor, the Church does its best to ensure there is no strife over the position.

Second, the apostles wanted to provide for future believers. To ensure the life of the Church—as well as the growth of the Church—successors had to be appointed. And note well, Clement tells us that the apostles instructed the churches they established to appoint *new* bishops once those whom they had appointed died. Why? To ensure that proper succession would take place and that the community of believers would have solid leadership, a foundation upon which they could build their faith. In fact, as we'll see in a moment, the future of the Church depends completely upon apostolic succession, for if the authority of Christ is not present on earth, then who has the power to make decisions about what is proper to Christian faith and practice?

Just to round things off, let's recall our discussion about *sola Scriptura*. We noted that one of the problems with this Protestant doctrine is what we called the problem of the canon. How do Protestants know which books belong to the Bible? Where is the authoritative list? Who has the authority to provide such a list? No Protestant can offer a satisfactory answer to those questions. However, we Catholics can. We can say that Jesus gave Peter and the apostles the power to bind and loose, that this power was handed down to their successors, and therefore they have the authority of Christ to determine which books belong in the Bible, and which do not. And that's exactly how an authoritative list of the Bible came into being.

What is true for Scripture is true for all of Christianity. What are the followers of Christ to do when controversy arises? To whom do they turn for guidance, for resolution? Who has the authority to keep the Church unified, as Christ wills? It's the successors of the apostles, for they, as Clement said, are given for future believers.

SAINT IRENAEUS OF LYONS

Next, let's look at a long passage from the man who was perhaps the greatest theologian of the early Church, Saint Irenaeus of Lyons (d. 202). Much can be said about Irenaeus, but perhaps what is most interesting is his spiritual lineage: he was the disciple of Saint Polycarp, who himself was a disciple of Saint John the Apostle. This makes Irenaeus the spiritual grandchild of the Beloved Disciple—but it also gives him a detailed memory of the apostolic Church; his understanding of the Church is not based on logical deduction, but stories handed down from his spiritual grandfather. This fact is evident in his writings, which, as we'll see, shows a knowledge of the apostolic church that is not found in later writers.

> It would be too long to enumerate in such a volume as this the succession of all the churches.... [Let us point out] the successions of the bishops of the greatest and most ancient church known to all, founded and

organized at Rome by the two most glorious apostles, Peter and Paul, that church which has the tradition and the faith which comes down to us after having been announced to men by the apostles.

The blessed apostles [Peter and Paul], having founded and built up the church [of Rome], they handed over the office of the episcopate to Linus. Paul makes mention of this Linus in the epistle to Timothy [2 Tim. 4:21]. To him succeeded Anencletus, and after him, in the third place from the apostles, Clement was chosen for the episcopate. He had seen the blessed apostles and was acquainted with them. It might be said that he still heard the echoes of the preaching of the apostles and had their traditions before his eyes. And not only he, for there were many still remaining who had been instructed by the apostles. In the time of Clement, no small dissension having arisen among the brethren in Corinth, the Church in Rome sent a very strong letter to the Corinthians, exhorting them to peace and renewing their faith.... To this Clement, Evaristus succeeded ... and now, in the twelfth place after the apostles, the lot of the episcopate [of Rome] has fallen to Eleutherus. In this order, and by the teaching of the apostles handed down in the Church, the preaching of the truth has come down to us." (*Against Heresies*, 3:3:2–3)

What I love most about of this passage is the window it offers to the early Christian community. First, it's obvious that, of all of Peter's early successors, Clement held a certain level of prestige the others did not enjoy; that's the only reason Irenaeus would write that Clement "still heard the echoes of the preaching of the apostles and had their traditions before his eye." But it's comforting to read that he knew the apostles for himself, and that while he was pope, there were still many in the Church who had been taught by the apostles.

But what is of real importance for us is how Irenaeus singles out the Church of Rome in order to discuss apostolic succession. He points out that he does not have the space to show how every local church (of which there were thousands by the time Irenaeus wrote) can trace its heritage back to one of the apostles, and so he decides to focus on the Roman Church. But he doesn't choose Rome at random. Rather, he chooses Rome because it was the "greatest and most ancient church known to all." In a word, the Church of Rome holds a primacy unlike any other Church. Why? Because it was founded by "the two most glorious apostles, Peter and Paul."

This point opens a door that, unfortunately, we cannot enter—namely, that even though we speak of the pope as the successor of Peter, there is a deeper, mystical reality at work in the office of the pope. This reality focuses on the particular missions Peter and Paul held: Peter was "the apostle to the Jews," and Paul "the apostle to the Gentiles." In the Jewish mind, the world was made up of only Jews and Gentiles; there was no other division. So, from this viewpoint, Peter and Paul were sent to the entire world. Early Christian theology taught that the pope was sent to the entire world *because* he carried in him the missions of *both* Peter and Paul. This view is preserved today in the official liturgical prayers of the Church, but most Catholics are unaware of this connection. (For more information, see Farmer & Kereszty, *Peter and Paul in the Church of Rome*.)

But let us return to the passage at hand. Note well the connection Irenaeus makes between the Church in Rome, the apostles, and the truth of Christ. Irenaeus writes, "[Let us point out] the successions of the bishops of the greatest and most ancient church known to all, founded and organized at Rome ... that church which has the tradition and the faith which comes down to us after having been announced to men by the apostles." And a little bit later, after listing the succession of the Bishops of Rome from Peter and Paul down to Eleutherus, he adds that it is because of this succession that "the teaching of the apostles [is] handed down in the Church, [and] the preaching of the truth has come down to us."

Thus, in Saint Irenaeus, we see a focus on the Roman Church, which means a focus on the Bishops of Rome—all of whom are successors of Peter (and Paul). This is important, for it shows that by the mid-to-late second century, the Christian world was focused on Rome because that's where the successor of Peter held office. For Irenaeus, to be in union with Rome is to be connected with the apostolic tradition of faith and the preaching of the truth of Christ.

SAINT CYPRIAN OF CARTHAGE

Finally, we turn our attention to Saint Cyprian of Carthage (d. 258), a highly influential North African bishop who was beheaded for refusing to offer sacrifice to pagan gods. In his book on the unity of the Church, he says that a person can only be united to the Church of Christ if they are united to Peter.

> The Lord says to Peter, "I say to you, you are Peter and upon this rock I will build my Church and the gates of hell will not overcome it. And to you I will give the keys of the kingdom of heaven and whatever you bind on earth, shall be bound also in heaven, and whatever you loose on earth, shall be loosed also in heaven." And again he says to him after His resurrection, "Feed my sheep." On him, he builds the Church and to him, he gives the command to feed the sheep. And although he assigns a similar power to all the other apostles, yet he founded a single chair and he established by his own authority a source and an intrinsic reason for that unity. Indeed, the others were also, that which Peter was, but the primacy is given to Peter, whereby it is made clear how there is but one church and one chair. So too, all our shepherds and the flock, is shown to be one, that by all the apostles in single-minded accord. If

someone does not build fast on this unity of Peter, can he imagine that he still holds the faith? If he deserts the chair of Peter upon whom the church was built, can he still be confident that he is in the church? (*The Unity of the Catholic Church*, no. 4)

The word "chair" (*cathedra* in Latin) is the key to understanding this passage. Even though there is a physical "Chair of Peter" inside of St. Peter's Basilica, Cyprian is not speaking of any actual chair that Peter used, or of any chair the pope sits in. Rather, he is using the word "chair" as we do when we speak of the chair of the board, the chair of an academic department, or the editorial chair of a publishing company. The chair of Peter is not an object, but an official position of authority. Like all official positions of authority, it must be filled. When the one who holds the chair dies (or resigns), another must take his place. Thus, the chair of Peter is a position with successors, each of whom holds the authority of Christ given to Peter. This was the belief of Christians in the first part of the third century.

But Cyprian is pointing to more than papal authority and succession. He reminds us that Peter is *the* rock upon which Christ builds his Church. While all of the apostles (and their successors) have authority, there is only *one* rock, only *one* chair, which gives the office of the pope a singular authority—the authority to establish unity.

In the Nicene Creed, we say that we believe in "one,

holy, catholic, and apostolic Church." Much can be said about each of these adjectives, but let's focus on the first —that the Church is one. How is the Church, which is spread across time, across cultures, and across the globe, how is this Church one? What gives unity to the Church? Saint Cyprian gives us the answer: "single-minded accord" of what she believes to be true. That's another way of saying that the Church is unified by her faith. But what if there are disputes? What if there are dissensions? What if bishops themselves, who are successors to the apostles, disagree about what authentic Christian faith and practice look like? How does the Church remain one; how is unity maintained?

Again, Cyprian gives us the answer: "If someone does not build fast on this unity of Peter, can he imagine that he still holds the faith? If he deserts the chair of Peter upon whom the church was built, can he still be confident that he is in the church?" The pope is the one who unites the Church, for the pope has the power to bind, to loose, and to teach with the authority of Christ himself. Those who are united to the pope are united to the Church, and those who are united to the Church are united to Christ. But to reject the authority of the pope is to reject the authority of Christ. This is why Saint Cyprian also said: "He can no longer have God for his Father who has not the Church for his mother." The pope is the one in whom Christ's will for unity is fulfilled.

What you're really saying is that Jesus intended for there to be a pope from the moment he made Peter the rock on which he would build his Church. That means the pope isn't just a "Catholic thing," but, rather, that he's an essential part of Christ's teaching, right?

When we don't understand the biblical and historical background of Church teaching, it's easy to see it as "Catholic teaching" and not as essential to the gospel of Jesus Christ. But the deeper we get into theology, the more obvious that the saving message of Christ is much, *much* broader than a mere surface-level reading of the New Testament.

But, also, if you consider what the office of the pope ensures the community of believers, it's obvious that God intended Peter to be the first of many popes. If the words and deeds of Christ—if his teaching, death, and resurrection—are essential for salvation, there *must* be a way to ensure that this message is free from every error for all generations. If not—if the message of salvation can be distorted—then why did God become man, teach us, and die for us? What would be the point, if all that Jesus said and did was not preserved from error and misunderstanding?

How does God preserve the message of salvation? Protestants say that it is preserved without error in Sacred Scripture. To that, every Catholic agrees (*Cate-*

chism, no. 107). But we disagree with the Protestant doctrine of *sola Scriptura*, that the Bible is the *sole* authority for Christian faith and practice. We have already provided some reasons why this cannot be the case, but there is another reason we've yet to mention. If Protestantism is correct—if the Bible is the sole authority for Christianity—why are there 200 official Protestant denominations and upward of 30,000 independent and non-denomination Protestant communities in the United State (see Beale, "Just How Many Protestant Denominations Are There?")? The best argument against Protestantism is Protestantism itself, for surely the one God did not intend his people to be divided into 30,000 different communities, each with their own particular doctrines and practices.

The reality is good people can read the Bible and come to different conclusions as to what it means. Good people can reflect on the death and resurrection of Christ and interpret it differently. And given the fact that we are 2,000 years removed from Christ and his apostles —and given the fact that we are not reading the Bible in its original languages—it is impossible for us to know exactly what original Christianity looked like from the Bible alone. It seems to me that it's not too far off the mark to say that Protestants remake the church of the apostles in their own likeness. But shouldn't it be the other way around? Shouldn't the Church of the apostles be remaking us in its likeness, which is the likeness of Christ?

So: how does God preserve the message of salvation? The Catholic Church says that it is preserved in three ways—by Sacred Scripture, Sacred Tradition, and the Magisterium, which is composed of the pope and all the bishops who are in union with the pope. Reread that final clause and note the role of the pope. He stands at the center of the Church's teaching authority. In the final analysis, the pope guarantees the unity of faith. He guarantees that the message of Christ is free from all error. This error can come in different ways; doctrine and practice can be removed, added, or distorted. In every case, the pope guarantees that error will not distort the message of Christ, and he guarantees that the message of Christ will be proclaimed in its fullness to every generation.

If we had time, we could talk about how the canon of New Testament, the date of Easter, the full divinity *and* full humanity of Christ, and the personhood *and* divinity of the Holy Spirit were all preserved by the authority of the pope. And if you reread that list, you'll see that I've not listed any doctrine particular to the Catholic Church. Whether Protestants know it or not—whether they accept it or not—the most basic of *all* Christian teachings they hold as bedrock biblical truths have endured only because of a successor of Saint Peter.

EPILOGUE

And so we reach the end of our first study. My goal was to help you establish firm foundations for your faith in God, Christ, and the Church. I hope I succeeded.

Faith and reason must work together in our pursuit of truth, and for faith to be fully realized, it must have deep roots in the soil of logic and reason. Therefore, we developed rational grounds for believing that God exists, that Jesus of Nazareth has been raised from the dead, and that the Catholic Church is the one true Church established by Christ.

But I should note that, with all of these topics, we've only scratched the surface. Longer books than this one have been written about the existence of God, about why Jesus of Nazareth is who he said he is, and about the truth of Catholicism. I never intended to provide you with every possible argument for each, but, rather, to show you how they are connected.

Does this mean you can to use this book to lead a person from atheism into the Catholic Church? Probably not. While this book does provide you with the roadmap, giving you the tools to convert others was never my goal. At one point in time, I wanted to be a Catholic apologist, but the Lord led me down a different path—the path of theological catechesis.

I've already mentioned my primary goal for this book: to help you establish firm foundations for your faith. Why is this important? Because doubt is all around us, and we cannot but help being affected by it—particularly when we are going through rough times. That's when we're most vulnerable to the temptations of the evil one. Saint Peter tells us the "devil is prowling around like a roaring lion looking for someone to devour" (1 Peter 5:8, *New American Bible*). And Jesus tells us that the devil actively tries to snatch the Word of God from our minds and hearts whenever we hear it (Matthew 13:19). It's important for us to know how to resist the devil and defend ourselves against his attacks. We need to pray, yes, but, as Peter tells us, we also resist the devil by being strong in our faith (1 Peter 5:9).

I strongly encourage you to continue your study by reading books that will strengthen the foundations of your faith. Always be ready to answer these three questions: Why do I believe in God? Why do I believe in Christ? Why do I believe in the Church? Answering them is not only the beginning of our study, they also will bring new dimensions to your relationship with Jesus Christ.

And you can be sure that Christ is calling you to a deeper relationship with him. I know this to be true because you have read this book, and anyone who reads a book like this one is responding to the call of Christ—the call to know him better and love him more.

And when you consider how few Catholics know their faith, you will realize just how precious this call really is.

BIBLIOGRAPHY

Barnett, Paul. *Is the New Testament Reliable?* Revised Edition. Downers Grove: IVP Academic, 2003.

Barron, Robert. *Catholicism: A Journey to the Heart of Faith.* New York: Image Books, 2001.

Beale, "Just How Many Protestant Denominations Are There?" NCRegister.com.

Benedict XVI. *God Is Love (Deus Caritas Est).* 2005. Vatican website.

_____. *Jesus of Nazareth: From the Baptism in the Jordan to the Transfiguration.* New York: Doubleday, 2007.

_____. *Jesus of Nazareth: Holy Week.* New York: Doubleday, 2011.

Chaput, Charles J. *Strangers in a Strange Land: Living the Catholic Faith in a Post-Christian World*. New York: Henry Hold and Company, 2017.

Escrivá, Josemaría. *The Way*. London: Scepter, 1982.

Farmer, William and Kereszty, Roch. *Peter and Paul in the Church of Rome*. New York: Paulist Press, 1990.

Graham, Henry G. *Where We Got the Bible: Our Debt to the Catholic Church*. Charlotte: TAN Books, 2010.

Hahn, Scott, ed. *Catholic Bible Dictionary*. New York: Doubleday, 2000.

_____. *Why Do We Have a Pope?* Audio CD. Lighthouse Catholic Media.

Hardon, John. *Biblical Spirituality Retreat*. Father John A. Hardon Audio Archives, 098. TheRealPresence.org.

_____. *Modern Catholic Dictionary*. Bardstown: Eternal Life, 2004.

_____. *Advanced Catholic Catechism Course*. Bardstown: Eternal Life, 2005.

Ignatius of Loyola. *Exercises*. Translated by Louis J. Puhl. Chicago: Loyola Press, 1951.

John Paul II. *On Catechesis in Our Time* (*Catechesi Tradendae*). 1979. Vatican website.

———. *On Faith and Reason* (*Fides et Ratio*). 1998. Vatican website.

Kereszty, Roch. *Jesus Christ: The Fundamentals of Christology*. New York: Alba House, 1991.

Kiger, "How Did the Apostles Die?" *NationalGeographic.com*.

Martin, James. *My Life with the Saints*. Chicago: Loyola Press, 2007.

Pitre, Brant. *The Case for Jesus: The Biblical and Historical Evidence for Christ*. New York: Image Books, 2016.

Prat, Ferdinand. *Jesus Christ: His Life, His Teaching, and His Work*. Volume 2. New York: The Bruce Publishing Company, 1950.

Sheed, Frank. *To Know Christ Jesus*. San Francisco: Ignatius Press, 1992.

ACKNOWLEDGMENTS

All books are written in isolation, but they are refined with help from others. Here are those who helped me.

Denny Haney, Kathy and Tim McCormick, Annie Watson, and Debbie Wilfong read this book in its manuscript form, and each offered invaluable comments as to how to make it better.

Mary Emery edited this book with a keen eye.

Father Roger Morgan, of the Diocese of Charleston, read over this book for both doctrinal and theological accuracy.

Any mistakes still found within these pages are mine, and mine alone.

I'd like to thank my four children for taking an interest in—and praying for—their father's "mission."

Finally, my deepest thanks goes to my wife, Monica, for all her love and support. She believed when I didn't.

Jeff Vehige holds a BA and MA in theology from the University of Dallas. For nearly twenty years, he has taught a wide variety of classes in the areas of Catholic doctrine, Sacred Scripture, the sacraments, and the spiritual life. He was an RCIA Director, a Catechist Formation Instructor for the Diocese of Dallas, and the Theology Department Chair at St. Elizabeth Ann Seton Catholic High School in Myrtle Beach, South Carolina. Married with four children, Jeff is the founder of the Find the Faith Apostolate.

ABOUT FIND THE FAITH

Find the Faith is a Catholic teaching apostolate that promotes a life-changing study of Catholic doctrine. The apostolate seeks to serve Catholics by offering a "theological catechesis" of the faith.

The apostolate's primary goal is to walk through the body of Catholic teaching by focusing on the four pillars of the faith—the creed, the liturgy and sacraments, morality, and prayer. To do this well, its secondary goal is to teach people how to think theologically and philosophically and to provide them with the biblical and historical foundations of Catholic doctrine.

The apostolate has two main modes of teaching: the Find the Faith book series and the Find the Faith podcast. Both complement one another, and both are intended to reach as many Catholics as possible.

FindTheFaith.com

Made in the USA
Middletown, DE
17 April 2018